COTTAGE GARDEN
FLOWERS

COTTAGE GARDEN FLOWERS

Margery Fish

with a foreword by
Fred Whitsey, Editor of
Popular Gardening

faber and faber
LONDON · BOSTON

First published in 1961 by
W. H. & L. Collingridge Limited
Reissued in 1970 by
David & Charles (Publishers) Limited
First published in Faber Paperbacks in 1980
by Faber & Faber Limited
3 Queen Square London WC1N 3AU
Reprinted in 1985 and 1989
Printed and bound in Great Britain by
Richard Clay Ltd Bungay Suffolk
All rights reserved

ISBN 0 571 11462 8

Contents

Illustrations

A typical cottage medley
Apples, tomatoes and dahlias flourish among flowers
Cottagers and their gardens
Helxine solierolii
Saxifraga umbrosa
Peony officinalis
Raised borders well filled with plants
Roses surround the windows of a cottage
A cottage in a woodland setting
Clumps of lavender beside a stone path
A generous mixture of cottage flowers
Hollyhocks and handsome conifers

Foreword

In the world of gardeners greatness is signified by the mode of address. Composers, writers, artists among the worthies may be known simply by their surnames. Mozart, Dickens, Renoir yes: but, even though they have long left us, always Mr. Bowles, Miss Jekyll – Mrs. Fish. It is as though they were still about and deserving our polite respect.

Margery Fish is one of the undoubted immortals of gardening. She was both of her time and made her time. When labour saving in the garden was the current vogue, as though the craft were some penance to be endured, when shrubs were all the thing and we were bidden to plant nothing else for fear of making work, she entered our world and proved a luminary among us. She revived and introduced to us the innumerable joys of the forgotten heaven of cottage garden plants. Some grew wildly. But others needed to be coaxed to persuade them to grow. All deserved and repaid intimate acquaintance as individuals. They restored variety to gardens which, under the influence of the no bother school were in danger of becoming dull and impoverished of flowers, unembellished by the detail which the endearing plants of the cottage garden can bestow.

Mrs. Fish's preoccupation with little plants in what I can only think of now, in Donne's powerful phrase, as 'numberless infinities' was incredible and infectious. Her enthusiasm was boundless and reached out far and wide. How she ever kept track of all she grew, how she came to know each one with the close intimacy she did, is past understanding. How did she ever find the time? Her era as a gardener was so short in plantsman's terms. It spanned a mere twenty years, for she did not begin until well into middle life. Twenty springs she had in her garden, twenty summers' flowering, twenty winters in which to prepare for the next season.

So brief a career. Yet it was enough for her revelation to be accomplished. Like Blake she taught us to 'see not with the eye but through the eye'. And still does through the enchanting pages of her books.

Fred Whitsey
1980

8

Introduction

Nowhere in the world is there anything quite like the English cottage garden. In every village and hamlet in the land there were these little gardens, always gay and never garish, and so obviously loved. There are not so many now, alas, as those cottages of cob or brick, with their thatched roofs and tiny crooked windows, are disappearing to make way for council houses and modern bungalows, but the flowers remain, flowers that have come to be known as 'cottage flowers' because of their simple, steadfast qualities.

The gardens themselves were usually small, sometimes only a slip between the cottage and the road, with a tiny patch behind. They were tidy without being prim and were always packed with flowers.

No definite design went to their planting and the treasured flowers were put wherever there was room. There might be a myrtle, grown from a sprig from grandmother's wedding bouquet, pinks from coveted slips, rosemary and Lad's Love, the great red peonies that last so well, and Crown Imperials grown in a row. Wallflowers and Snapdragons grew in the walls, and cheerful red and pink daisies played hide and seek between the shells that edged the path.

Plants are friendly creatures and enjoy each other's company. The close-packed plants in a cottage garden grow well and look happy. They have the shelter of the wall or hedge that screens them from the road, and the comfortable backing of cabbages and leeks. Pansies and Forget-me-Nots flower under the currant bushes, nasturtiums frolic among the carrots, and old apple trees give welcome shade.

I am afraid the cottages and their little gardens may disappear completely as the years go by and we shall have to remember them by the flowers. The treasures that made those little gardens so irresistible for so many years must have toughness and determination as well as artless beauty. Great efforts are being made to preserve our old buildings, and we must also cherish the simple flowers that brightened our cottage gardens for so many years.

1. Spring Flowers

The flowers of spring open early in a cottage garden. They have been sheltered all through the winter with walls or hedge, and they get more protection from the plants growing near them.

Aconites and snowdrops will be peeping through in January. Sometimes there is grass outside the cottage gate or it may be on the other side of the road. Snowdrops will sow themselves in grass wherever they can and it is quite usual to see them growing happily in a grass bank opposite a cottage or peopling the rough grass verges along the road. Life in the road is dangerous with cattle passing regularly, and many a plodding foot must descend on those innocent heads, but it does not deter them. Up they come, year after year, with more every season, little white buds between spears of green. I always think they are holding up green hands to clasp the fragile buds and protect them as they push through the soil. Aconites sow themselves too, but not quite so regularly or generously.

Symphytum grandiflorum is not a spectacular plant but the foliage is evergreen and the little hanging flowers in cream, tipped with orange, flower in January. Its old name is 'Cherubin and Seraphim' and it is sensible to flower so early because we should not pay much attention to it later on. The foliage is at its best early in the year too. Always rough and dark it gets rather coarse by the end of the summer but it does not show much in the dark corners in which it likes to grow.

Violets have been blooming from November but they flower in earnest from February onwards, and there will be little orange crocuses springing up in odd corners.

Omphalodes verna is really an April flowerer but it usually cannot wait till then. I often see a little blue eye looking up at me in really wintry February weather when all good children should be asleep. There is more than a suggestion of pink about

11

these early flowers and when they come to their official opening
they are the bluest of the blue. In fact Blue-Eyed Mary is the
name it goes by. This is said to have been Marie Antoinette's
favourite flower and I believe it grew wild in the woods near
Schönnbrun in Austria. Although its flowers are so lovely and
contrast so well with the pointed hairy leaves it is rather untidy
in its growth. It makes long stems with the little rosettes of
leaves and flowers at the end of them, and a few tattered brown
leaves on the way. It really needs to be grown in a mass to be
effective but in a cottage garden the other plants conceal the
ugly bare stems and we enjoy the little blue flowers tumbling
among the herbage.

There are other omphalodes; *O. cappadocica*, rejoices in the
name of Blue-Eyed Betty. It is much neater in growth and makes
a good clump of very elegant smooth pointed leaves above which
we have those dainty sprays of such very blue flowers. Why is it,
I wonder, that blue flowers give such a feeling of innocence and
simplicity? In a small garden this omphalodes takes up very little
room. It can be wedged at the side of a path or planted to hang
over a wall. It is much easier to propagate than *O. verna*, because
the clumps can be broken into many fragments, each with a good
crop of fine roots. I do not know if there is a white form of *O.
cappadocica*. I have never seen one, but I have a white *Omphalodes
verna* and it is very lovely.

Solomon's Seal (*Polygonatum multiflorum major*) is a favourite cottage plant which has enjoyed a real come back. I think
we have the flower arrangers to thank for this (but I wish they
would not take off the leaves as they do for some of their
arrangements) and also the changing taste in many gardeners.
Instead of planning our gardens for a riot of colour we seek satis-
faction in textures, neutral shades and green in every tone. The
hanging green-tipped bells of Solomon's Seal, with spreading
leaves above, are grace personified. To see them at their best I
think they should be planted at the top of a bank—something it
would be difficult to do in a tiny cottage garden, but they can
arch from the corner of a bed. There seem to be two distinct
forms of this plant, the one most usually grown, which is about
three feet high, and another which is about a foot. For the connoisseur there is a double flowered form, which, quite honestly

is not so beautiful as that with single flowers, then there is *P. oppositifolium* with rather smaller flowers and two tiny ones, *P. falcatum* a few inches high is white, and *P. hookeri*, pink. The Solomon's Seal with variegated leaves is very rare but most exciting when you find it.

There must be some Biblical association with this plant because it is also called David's Harp as well as Lady's Seal. Not only is it beautiful in flower but afterwards there are lovely berries. At first they are green and very decorative, and then they turn black, with a bloom of blue. When ripe they are as big as ivy berries and, according to old writers, have a very sweet and pleasant taste—but I have not had the courage to put this to the test. At one time the roots of Solomon's Seal were recommended as a cure for bruises.

Early in the century Crown Imperials (*Fritillaria imperialis*) were grown in many gardens. I know we had them in the first garden I can remember and it was not in any way a connoisseur's collection. But interest in them dwindled and now we usually have to go to a cottage garden to find them. I regularly pass a little garden in a village on my way to Bath, where there is a magnificent row of tawny Crown Imperials. Not only do they make an imposing picture when seen from the road, but the flowers have great individuality. I like to lift up those handsome heads to look into their faces and to see if each has its customary drop of clear water, and it invariably has.

They are among the oldest flowers we have. Parkinson wrote about them in 1629. There were evidently many more varieties in his day as he says 'wherof some are white, others blush, some purple others red or yellow, some spotted, others without spots, some standing upright, others hanging or turning downwards'.

Nowadays we have only yellow or orange, and sometimes these are difficult to find. Mr Bowles had one with variegated leaves and that still grows in the garden of Myddleton House.

Crown Imperials need plenty of food. Manure should be added to the soil in which they are planted and more added when the stems are coming through. This helps the plant to produce new bulbs.

At one time some formal gardens were kept gay by filling the beds with fibre and sinking in it pots of flowers throughout the year, and in the winter evergreen plants. The Crown Imperials, brought on in the greenhouse, flowered a fortnight before those grown in the open and were a favourite subject.

Though there was a mania for growing tulips in earlier years, it was the elaborately marked types that were cultivated. The growers had no use for self-coloured flowers and these discarded types came into the possession of the cottagers, who certainly had no money to pay for the expensive bulbs. Now there is a definite class of tulip that goes by the name of 'cottage'. They are usually rather dwarf, simple unassuming flowers, but I have never really known what constitutes a 'cottage' tulip. My hazard is that any nice plain tulip that is not a species or a Darwin or a lily or a parrot or any other of the special types now grown is called, for want of a better name, a cottage tulip. I think it is a good name for they are simple and easy, they have good colour and strong constitutions, and very often they are scented, and what more could you ask of any flower?

I have always had great affection for that most typically cottage of all spring flowers, Bleeding Heart or Lyre Plant (*Dicentra spectabilis*). At one time it was so ordinary and so typical of the humbler gardens that it was rather dropped by more sophisticated gardeners. But not now. We have come to realise the grace and charm of its delicate foliage and the arching sprays of delicious pink flowers, with lyre-shaped petals which can be pulled back to reveal the little white lady modestly having her bath. Dicentra does so well in cottage gardens because it has shelter and peace. Although hardy in most positions it is too fragile to be buffeted by cold winds and its roots are very brittle and cannot bear to be disturbed.

Every spring for many years I used to enjoy wonderful dicentras in a cottage garden in the next village. They bloomed for many weeks and were a wonderful sight planted against the cottage wall of mellow hamstone. I miss them very much now that the cottage has changed hands and has taken on the qualities of a villa and the garden neatly planted with geraniums and white alyssum, spaced out along the house and at each side of the path.

A great fuss is made of the dwarf dicentras, the new *D. eximia* Bountiful and the ordinary pink and white forms, which make such excellent subjects for growing under trees or among shrubs. They are all very pretty and flower for a long time, but they have not the character or grace of our old friend the Bleeding Heart.

Walking round a cottage garden in late spring you may spy a dazzling dome of greeny-gold and may wonder what it is. Doronicums, simple, easy and effective, are long since over, although they made a patch of glinting gold early in the year. On closer inspection the rounded clump turns out to be *Euphorbia epithymoides* or *E. polychroma* and the gold comes from the conspicuous bracts behind the tiny flowers. Whatever its name it is a captivating plant, with its compact shape and glistening radiance, and I think will grow in popularity. Unfortunately it does not seem to have the habit of generous seeding, and I have never found a single infant round my plants. Autumn cuttings do not succeed but anyone who can bear to remove the stubby little shoots as soon as they are a few inches long can have a nice batch of plants by the autumn.

Later in the summer the Creeping Euphorbia, *E. cyparissias*, may be filling a shady corner with delicate green. The country name for this plant is Ploughman's Mignonette—but it really looks more like a little green cypress with a small head of golden bracted flowers. Tidy minded gardeners are sometimes frightened to let it in the garden because it is inclined to run. It has been known to run like mad, but if it is planted where it cannot get up to much mischief it can be enjoyed without reservations. I have a friend who put a scrap in a shaded piece of paving, and very soon it had popped up in every crevice it could find. But it was limited by the size of the paving, and when it got too thick she pulled out handfuls and left it to repeat the performance. In addition to the greeny-yellow flowers on their shaggy green stems, that delight us early in the year, in the autumn it turns a glorious red.

It always surprises me that the little *Ornithogalum umbellatum*, commonly known as Star of Bethlehem, flowers so late in the spring. In one's mind it is a spring bulb, which it is but it is late spring, almost the end of May, when it opens its white starry flowers, growing polyanthus fashion on a short stalk, all delicately marked with green. It comes up regularly year after year where it is left alone, so the place to grow it is in grass that is not too coarse—or in a cottage garden.

One of the first flowers to greet the spring is *Pulmonaria officinalis*, a humble member of the borage family. And how welcome are those jaunty sprays of innocent flowers in blue and pink, often rising above the snow, and fluttering unconcernedly in the bitter winds of March. The common name is Lungwort, from *pulmo*, a lung, as the plant was used in the old days to cure lung disease. But, like other popular plants, that is only one of many names. The little pink and blue flowers growing together reminded someone of the old saying 'pink for a girl and blue for a boy' so we have Boys and Girls as one name, and Soldiers and Sailors for another. In Somerset they like Bloody Butcher, going back to the days when every self-respecting butcher wore a striped blue apron round his portly person. More romantic is Hundreds and Thousands, for a big clump of pulmonaria is a delightful medley of pastel tints. Another old name is Joseph and Mary, why I do not know.

Pulmonaria officinalis was the one grown in most cottage gardens, with heart-shaped, spotted leaves, as rough as a calf's tongue, with blue and pink flowers growing together. The white flowered form is icy and aloof and may be too pure for those who like richness of colour in their flowers.

Pulmonarias are very popular today with our liking for handsome foliage and good ground cover, but connoisseurs are choosy about them. They want the one known as *P. saccharata* because its leaves are longer and more heavily spotted. Collecting good forms is a regular gardening sport, and some of those found are so heavily covered with spots that they are practically silver. There is one good pulmonaria in this family called *P. saccharata* Mrs Moon, with very good foliage and flowers that open pink then turn to blue, but I have never found out who Mrs Moon was or where she lived.

The red Pulmonaria *P. rubra* comes out very early, often before the blue and pink. It is a fine reward for facing the draughty air of a February day to come face to face with little clusters of tight coral flowers tucked into cups of soft green foliage. *Pulmonaria rubra* has no markings on its leaves and the flowers are the brightest shade of pure coral. Sometimes this plant is called Bethlehem Sage, and I have heard country folk refer to it as the Christmas Cowslip. There is a particularly good form known as Mr Bowles' Red. It does not appear to be very different from the ordinary type except that the habit is a little more upright and the flowers a little brighter and bigger, and is just another example of the late Mr Bowles' unerring eye for a good plant.

The blue Pulmonarias are a little higher in the social scale and are sometimes considered worthy of a place in a rock garden. There is a little confusion about the names. *P. angustifolia* appears to be the same as *P. azurea* with *P. angustifolia azurea* as the name for one with light-blue flowers. They divide again into Mawson's Blue and Munstead Blue, but I have never found anyone yet who can find much difference between them. I prefer Munstead Blue, which must have come from Miss Gertrude Jekyll's garden, and is, I think, a more refined plant. It is deciduous and slow-growing. The leaves appear before the flowers as little folded pricks of bright green, and the intensely blue flowers are carried on six inch stems. The leaves of Mawson's Blue seem to last all the year and the flowers do not appear quite so spectacular with such a background of rough dark green.

Pulmonarias seed quite generously and the clumps can be divided as they grow bigger. Though these plants look right anywhere in a cottage garden they need more careful placing in a larger sphere. They are perfect in a wild or woodland garden, for their leaves get bigger as the season advances and compete successfully with the toughest grass. And for that reason they do not merit a front line position in the flower garden, where their coarse foliage will displease later in the year. They are a real pleasure in the spring garden and if they can be planted at the back of the border, against a wall or hedge, their bright little faces can be enjoyed with the knowledge that when the tiny leaves of babyhood grow coarse with middle-age they will blend and become absorbed with the summer growth of the other plants in the border.

2. Sweet Smelling Herbs

Every cottage garden had its big bush of rosemary either just inside the gate or beside the front door. In very old cottage gardens the bush reaches the bedroom windows and melts into the thatch. Whether by accident or design, the bushes always seem to be in the line of traffic so that the inmates brush against them many times a day and release the pungent, penetrating scent that is so typical of a cottage garden.

Sometimes the plants would have flowers of a specially good colour, grown from a cutting from the 'big garden', but usually it was the ordinary type, *Rosmarinus officinalis*, just rosemary, but a much loved bush nevertheless; sprigs were given at partings, to be pressed between the leaves of the Bible, a tiny bunch, tied with ribbon, was placed in every coffin, and, more prosaically, linen was spread to dry on the old rosemary bush. The sun brought out the astringent scent and imparted it to the linen. An infusion of the plant, camphor and southernwood was sometimes made for washing the hair. The scientific name derives from the Latin 'ros' (dew) and 'marinus' (of the sea).

I wonder if the golden variegated form we grow today is the same as the Gilded Rosemary that Parkinson wrote about in 1629? I think this may well be so—for that plant, for all its pretty name, had a sickly appearance. The golden variegated rosemary I grow is rather a flimsy plant, with spidery leaves and weak stems. The golden variegations of this var. *aureus* are not very marked, they seem to come and go but at their best they do give the plant a 'gilded' look. There was once a silver striped rosemary but I do not know if it exists today. I have read about it but have never seen it. Perhaps it is still growing in some small and forgotten garden.

Scented leaves were typical of the plants that filled our cottage gardens. I do not know if their inmates used Balm (*Melissa*

18

officinalis) to make tea or to dry for scenting linen, but there would always be a plant in the garden, no doubt several plants, for it is an inveterate seeder. I have always had Balm in my garden but I try to limit myself to one or two plants. I thought golden Balm might behave itself better, but I have not noticed any reticence in its child producing ways. Again I wonder if my golden Balm is the one mentioned by R. Morison in 1680. Mine is mildly variegated with gold, not really enough to warrant the use of the word 'golden', as it is more rusty than glittering.

'Balm of Gilead', a name also applied to a poplar (*P. gileadensis*) but here referring to a Sage (*Cedronella triphylla*), is not completely hardy but it scrapes through most winters, particularly if it is grown in a sheltered spot or in a thickly planted garden. Why the name I do not know. It came from the Canary Islands in 1697 and has been lurking in humble little gardens ever since. Its flowers in mauve or white are pretty without being striking, but its leaves are pleasantly scented when lightly bruised. It used to be popular for foliage in buttonholes, because as the leaves fade they give off whiffs of scent.

Different kinds of mint (*mentha*) were treasured for their varying scents and uses. The dark leaved Spear-mint (*M. spicata*) was harvested and dried. Mint tea was a trusted remedy for winter colds and sore throats. Eau de Cologne mint (*Mentha × piperita* var. *citrata*) was used at one time, I believe, to make toilet water. It is an old plant and is found in the old gardens where it scents the air and adds perfume to potpourri and folded linen. Bergamot mint is another form and is rather similar, but has slightly smaller, paler leaves and a scent that combines that of bergamot with a suspicion of mixed herbs.

It is a pity that these mints spread so rapidly but I think we should profit by their generosity and plant them in some place where they can ramp and where we walk, so that we brush against them and enjoy their fragrance many times a day. In a herb garden they can be planted in drain pipes or bottomless oil-drums to prevent them from overrunning everything else.

Apple mint has large leaves which are greyer and more furry than the other mints. Its scent and flavour are cleaner and sharper and it is particularly favoured for flavouring new peas and new potatoes, while the ordinary green mint (*M. spicata* syn. *M. viridis*) has no equal for mint sauce.

I do not know how one uses *Mentha* × *gentilis*, which I believe is the 'Cow Basil' mentioned by Gerard. The scent is more haunting and less culinary than the others and the leaves exude their delicate fragrance without being touched. I have this mint in its golden form in several places in the garden and I notice the scent whenever I am working nearby, even in the winter when there are only bare stems to show where it is growing. I planted it in several places where I wanted the beauty of its golden leaves and now I have difficulty in controlling it. All the mints have very determined roots but the long white thrusting roots of *M.* × *gentilis* are the most determined of them all. I believe this mint was used as a pot plant in cottage windows in Cheshire and Somerset, and I always wonder how those vigorous roots could be content to live in a pot.

There is something very refreshing about the scent of mint, and I have noticed how old country women like to pick a sprig in passing, particularly of eau de Cologne mint, and crush and squeeze as they talk.

Enjoyment of the scent of chamomile is an acquired taste, I always think, but the plants themselves are often pretty. I do not think even cottage folk would allow the yellow chamomile (*Anthemis tinctoria*) in their gardens. This plant, which comes up in such profusion on ground where there have been chickens, is quite pretty, but it has not the charm of Feverfew (*Chrysanthemum parthenium*) with its white flowers and rather yellow cut foliage. It makes a very neat, bushy little plant, and a few plants will nearly always be found in a cottage garden. I think it shows that these gardeners realise the value of a plant when everyone else scorns it. Now an improved form of *Chrysanthemum parthenium* has appeared and is taking its place among the ranks of high-class plants. The flowers are much bigger than in the wild plant, they are a very full double and the snowy petals take on a green tinge in the centre of each flower. It calls itself 'White Bonnet' and I foresee for it a great future. It is one of those simple, attractive plants that grow as if they enjoyed it and which flower right up to December.

The scent of the creeping chamomile (*Anthemis nobilis*) is far

pleasanter than that of the bushy types. I have heard it likened to
apples. The apple scent is there but there is another less distinct
scent mingled with it. The foliage of this plant is a brilliant green
and it is quite tough, in spite of its fine texture. This is the plant
that is used for chamomile lawns and one really needs to walk
on it to get its full fragrance. The flowers are used for hair wash
and insomnia tea and it makes an excellent plant for filling in
spaces in paving.

To grow the double-flowered creeping chamomile well, I
think one needs a properly prepared site. In the past I have
poked bits into pavement crevices in my usual casual way, but it
has never taken kindly to the indignity; put it in nice rich soil,
which is fairly moist, and give it a top dressing of sand and peat
to start it off and there will very soon be a rich carpet of brilliant
green to delight the eye. How one is to get the scent without
bending down and pressing it with one's finger tips I do not
know. It would be very pleasant to sit on it. I often wonder if
the seat in Miss V. Sackville-West's herb garden at Sissinghurst
Castle is meant to be sat on? It is an old stone seat without a
seat, for the horizontal part is filled with earth and thickly
carpeted with *Mentha requienii.* This little plant emits the most
delicious scent of mint if one touches it. That growing on the seat
is at hand level and invites a passing brush if one has not the
temerity to sit on what is, after all, a planted flower bed.

Whenever I meet the scent of Southernwood (*Artemisia
abrotanum*) I am immediately taken right back to a little cottage
garden I knew well as a child. 'Delicious' is the adjective used
for the scent of Southernwood in nurserymen's catalogues, but I
would not call it delicious; it is aromatic and interesting and very
distinct, but to me not altogether pleasant. I would not want to
hold it and sniff it as I would mint. There is something rather
strange and fusty about it that reminds me of small airless
rooms full of old clothes. I am sure I am in the minority in this
for the cottagers love their 'Old Man', 'Lad's Love', or 'Boy's
Love', whichever they call it, far better than its better half the
Wormwood (*Artemisia absinthium*)—'Old Woman', which has a
clean and obvious tang. I can never detect any scent in 'Old
Warrior' (*A. pontica*) and the distinct horehound flavour of
Tarragon (*A. dracunculus*) is only discernible by biting a leaf.

All these artemisias are old and loved plants, judging by their names, but it is Southernwood that is most usually grown, and it is allowed to grow into a big bush which balances the rosemary bush. I always cut my Southernwood at ground level in the spring. In true cottage garden style I have a large plant just inside the gate, and it is one of my garden excitements to get rid of the old foliage and wait for the new fresh growth.

The inevitable lavender bush (*Lavandula spica*) would not be cut very drastically either. I am an offender here too. I know I should cut all my lavender drastically after it has finished flowering. That is the way to keep neat healthy bushes and get the maximum amount of flower. The plant can be grown in paving and clipped to any shape without being put out. My bushes are as large and shapeless as those in a cottage garden, they billow out over the path and make a nice mass of silver foliage. By now the stems are old and very woody and I am not brave enough to risk the really brutal cutting they need. Before I do it I must make a little nursery of cuttings so that all will not be lost if the poor old bushes cannot stand up to such cruel treatment.

To most of us lavender is just lavender, but for the expert there are over a dozen kinds from which to choose. 'Twickle Purple' is one of the oldest varieties we grow, with its rich purple flowers on long stalks. It is small and neat and so is 'Hidcot Purple'. I grow white and pink lavenders and the fascinating *Lavandula stoechas*, but not one of them has the rich, strong scent of the large ancient cottage garden plant.

In my childhood, every garden, big or little, had at least one bush of the Sweet-briars (*Rosa rubiginosa* etc.). I can smell it now, and it must be sixty years since I lived with a Sweet-briar. The showy Penzance briars have put the old plant in the shade but they do not give us that delicious perfume, which was almost overpowering after rain. It is a scent that it is impossible to describe, it has the crispness of green apples and the lingering fragrance of mint and something else all its own. Herb specialists still grow Sweet-briar and I cannot understand why I have never put a bush in my garden.

The Bergamots or Bee Balms, used to be in every garden. They are coming back into favour now and many new colours have appeared within the last few years. These are species and varieties of *monarda* that enjoy honoured places in many a noble border. The old plant of the cottage garden is the original *M. didyma*, of which 'Cambridge Scarlet' is an improved form. The old plant is rather different in structure from our modern types, a little heavier and less tall, with rather more green between the colour in its whorled flowers.

The foliage of Bergamot has a most beguiling perfume. It does not need to be picked or touched to fill the air around with its haunting fragrance. Even in the depths of winter it makes its presence known if one is working in a border where it grows, when very often there is scarcely a leaf showing. I always feel one ought to make more use of this gift from Heaven. True one can put a leaf in the teapot and change the flavour of ordinary tea to something quite exotic, a few sprigs among the sheets will give lasting fragrance, and it gives that necessary 'bite' to pot-pourri that nothing else can supply.

Costmary or Alecost (*Chrysanthemum balsamita balsamitoides*) was sometimes called 'mint geranium'. It was used to flavour mulled ale and chopped leaves were sometimes added to salad to give a mint flavour. The leaves are beautiful in themselves without their strong flavour of spearmint and I think a good clump of this plant is attractive in any garden. I like the little daisy flowers which, incidentally, last well in water. In olden days the plant was called 'Bible leaf' because a leaf put between the pages of one's Bible was sweet to smell in church. I have never experimented with *Chrysanthemum balsamita*, with its strong scent of camphor. It may be that it could be used among one's clothes to keep away moths.

Sweet Cicely (*Myrrhis odorata*) possesses a way of keeping itself in any garden to which it takes a fancy. It puts its seedlings in odd corners and one has not the heart to uproot that dainty ferny foliage. The plant boasts an anise scent and with its small white flowers on top of the feathery leaves it is quite attractive in any garden.

Woad is most attractive too. I think it is some years since it was grown to give our forebears blue dye but it has earned a place in our gardens by the beauty of its person. Common Dyer's Weed, *Isatis tinctoria*, to give it its full name, makes a good bushy plant about two feet high. Its foliage has a bluish tinge and it looks rather like a yellow flowered *crambe* when it is covered with its little golden flowers. When the flowers are over it is still beautiful for then its myriad branches drip with small black seeds, which are big in proportion to the flowers.

It always seems to be that we should introduce Sweet Wood-ruff (*Asperula odorata*) into our gardens, and the cottagers do. It likes a shady, fairly moist position and then it settles down very happily to cover the spot with thread-like foliage and tiny white flowers. 'Our Lady's lace' was its old name and now it is usually called just 'Lady's lace' or 'Lady's laces'. Its scent of new mown hay is delicious and its dainty elegance is a good background for more stolid plants. Pink Woodruff, with white flowers tinged yellowish-pink, is *A. taurina*.

3. Daffodils

The daffodils that grew in the old gardens are not those we usually buy today. With all the new varieties to tempt us it is difficult not to fill the spring garden with fresh types, and most of us succumb to a few new varieties every year. The cottagers are more loyal. In their gardens the old friends come up year after year and it never occurs to the owners to oust them, nor to lift and divide them. They increase, of course, but they do not seem to deteriorate.

I have known the little Tenby Daffodil (*Narcissus obvallaris*) all my life. It was given to my Mother when she was a comparatively young woman and she grew it in every garden she ever had, and now her daughters are doing the same. How old it is I do not know, nor do I know anything about its beginnings except that it is thought to be a native of England.

It is only recently that I have discovered the name of this little daffodil. We have always called it 'Mother's little daffodil' and did not attempt to go further than that. It is a perfect little miniature trumpet daffodil about a foot high, with trumpet and petals the same shade of bright yellow. It is sturdy and has good firm foliage. When it first comes out it brings spring into the garden. By the time the last flowers fade the sun is strong and there are many other plants in bloom. Then one feels, I fear, that it is perhaps a little too yellow, and there is a feeling that its position in the garden should not be too conspicuous but it should be tucked away somewhere with a nice green background and foreground. Years ago I planted some in the rock garden and it is that little colony that seem a little out of place when spring is almost summer. I give away a few bulbs now and then but they are now so deep in the ground that it is difficult to find them, and I feel it would be very ungrateful to take up the whole clump and put it in a less conspicuous place.

There is an old trumpet daffodil, raised as a hybrid long ago by a Lancashire weaver named John Horsfield, that used to be in every garden and which still survives in a few of the old tiny gardens, although it has disappeared from the lists of bulb growers. 'Horsfieldii' was popular before we had the incomparable 'King Alfred' and when that superb flower appeared of course it simply did not have a chance. I never felt that 'Horsfieldii' was a graceful plant even when there were few of our modern beauties with which to compare it. For one thing it is rather short for its heavy head, and for another the cream petals come down over the pale yellow trumpet instead of standing out bravely at right angles. It always reminds me of a man with shrugged shoulders and collar turned up trying to avoid the rain.

The 'Queen of Spain' goes to the other extreme, everything turns back and I always think of her as a frightened lady. It is, I believe, a wild hybrid of *Narcissus triandrus* and is not one of the easiest daffodils to keep so it is a miracle that it has survived to this day. A very old gardener was quite overcome when he saw it growing in a garden, the garden, in fact, from which I was given my bulbs. The "Queen of Spain", he said, leaning on his spade and mopping his face, The "Queen of Spain", 'I never thought I'd see the "Queen of Spain" again.'

It is a very refined little daffodil with a long narrow trumpet and recessed petals, all in a clear soft yellow.

Mr Bowles once had a colony of this daffodil below his rock garden. A year or two ago I went to Myddleton House and as I walked round with the gardener we looked for the 'Queen of Spain'. But she had gone. Someone may have stolen her in the interval after Mr Bowles' death or she may just have passed away through lack of attention. There were a few stray seedlings nearby which had some of the characteristics of the departed lady but not the cool aristocratic aloofness of the true queen.

There are other old single narcissi that are sometimes found, *N. poeticus* 'praecox' for instance, a very early species in a group that are late flowerers as a rule. This narcissus was at one time largely grown for market and it is cultivated in some old gardens—so is the polyanthus narcissus 'Soleil d'Or', so aptly named, with its orange cup and yellow petals. The old straw coloured jonquil 'Tenuior' is seldom seen now, although one reads about it in old gardening books.

The last of the single narcissus to flower, is, of course, the old Pheasant's eye, *N. poeticus recurvus*. I am always surprised when I see that this old friend still appears in modern catalogues, but I suppose its incomparable scent prevents it from being dropped. It is quite the most fragrant narcissus there is, although the flowers are rather small and thin according to modern standards. But the texture of the petals puts them in a separate class, for they have that same glittering quality that one finds in nerines and begonias, as if each tiny cell was encased with lenses to reflect the light.

I would always grow Pheasant's eye narcissi because of its scent and old associations, and crystalline purity, but it is a difficult plant to place. The foliage is little thicker than grass and it falls about in an untidy way. If I had long grass in which to grow it I think that would solve the problem, but as this is not the case I put it among shrubs and taller perennials so that one does not notice the leaves which are always bent and crumpled before the flowers appear. And what a long time it seems before they do appear. Each year I get in a panic that somehow I have lost all my Pheasant eye narcissi, even though those untidy leaves are staring me in the face. At last, when one has almost given up hope, its flowers do open and I think what an idiot I have been to think they would not.

When one thinks of old daffodils it is usually the double ones that come first to mind. They have an old world air and are the kind that seem to thrive without attention, and so we find them in the little old gardens that have daffodils next to the cabbages and tulips among the currants.

The earliest and the easiest is Van Sion, the old double daffodil. I am sure that all but the most erudite gardeners still feel that the flower with the big trumpet is a daffodil and the flat faced flowers with small crimped perianths are narcissi. It is no good telling us that daffodil is simply the English version of the Latin narcissus. I have read that daffodil may have been a derivation of asphodelus in the beginning, and it has several variations in the old books.

When the friendly Van Sion appears we are usually starved

for flowers and greet it with open arms. We do not notice that it is very yellow, that deep strong yellow that needs to be taken in small doses. It needs a generous green background and so is a perfect plant for naturalising, and with its iron constitution it will hold its own anywhere.

The old double white daffodil is much less violent, but it is also much less robust and increases slowly. It should, I think, be planted in shade, where its silvery white flowers show up well against a dark background. Like all the daffodils it likes to be planted in good soil but without manure. If you feel it needs a little encouragement a handful of bonemeal is always acceptable. The miniature daffodils planted in open beds are often top-dressed with a mixture of bonemeal and potash. Dusted on the surface of the soil in January it gets washed into the soil by the inevitable winter rains.

The little wild daffodil, or Lent lily, that still thrives in many parts of Britain, is one of the loveliest of our flowers. I imagine the rare double form, *N. pseudo-narcissus fl. plenus*, was a chance seedling. One sees it sometimes and it is worth chasing and cosseting when found. I am always glad that our little wild daffodils in their wild state protect themselves by being very deeply rooted. Luckily it is almost impossible to dig them up unless the marauders go armed with big spades. If it were not, I fear it would have disappeared by now. Owners of fields where Lent lilies grow reap a small harvest when they are in bloom by allowing motorists into the fields to gather the flowers. They do not come up with their roots as bluebells do and so are comparatively safe. Anyone who wants to grow wild daffodils can do so very easily and cheaply. They cost very little and they increase very fast, particularly if they are carefully planted in good soil.

A quaint little double form of *N. minor fl. plenus* goes under the name of Rip van Winkle. It is only 6 in. high and has a face like a small dandelion. How nice to have a dandelion flower that can be admired instead of being hounded out of the garden! There is something very beautiful about a dandelion and if it was a rare and difficult plant how we should rave about it! The trouble is that dandelions in the garden reflect on the gardener, and those handsome golden flowers are viewed through a nightmare veil of thousands of billowing 'clocks' floating away to settle in every corner of one's domain.

The late Mrs Clive told me once how a very ignorant visitor had been taken round her fabulous garden but of course found very few plants in it that were known to her. She wanted to pay a compliment on parting but not knowing the name of anything made it rather difficult. All she could find to say was 'You do grow wonderful dandelions', much to Mrs Clive's amusement.

The two most famous old double daffodils are attributed to Queen Anne, not Queen Anne of England as most of us assume, but Queen Anne of Austria. I expect both are still growing in old gardens where they have been for very many years; now, luckily, they can be bought, so we hope they will never die out.

It took me some time to get the real Queen Anne's daffodil as my first informant gave me the name of N. Pencrebar, which is a double jonquil and is known as 'Queen Anne's Jonquil', although I have read since that *N. jonquilla fl. pl.* is the real 'Queen Anne's Jonquil. N. Pencrebar is very beautiful and I was very pleased to have it but it was not the little cream flower I had seen in two gardens (one a Botanic Garden and the other the garden of a friend). Most old books agree that *N. capax plenus* (Syn. *N. eystettensis*) is the flower that was known as 'Queen Anne's Double daffodil'. It has been cultivated for at least three hundred years and must be sturdier than it looks. It is exquisitely fashioned with its petals arranged symmetrically so that it looks like a six pointed star. It seems to do best in moderate shade and in good soil enriched with bonemeal.

The last of all the double daffodils to flower is the double form of the Pheasant's eye narcissus, *N. poeticus fl. plenus*. It has the deliciously strong scent of Pheasant's eye and flowers even later. It is sometimes called the gardenia narcissus, because it looks almost like a gardenia. There are often traces of green in the flower, which makes it almost more exciting than the old Pheasant's eye, but the petals are flatter than those of the single flower and the luminous quality of the petals is not so noticeable.

I have seen it suggested that this is a good narcissus for naturalising but the friend who gave it to me said it must be planted in a bed, never in grass. So I grow mine in a narrow border under a hedge and look forward every year to the end of

May and early June when I can enjoy its old world flowers. Some years I do not get many flowers because the buds have been destroyed by a late frost. It seems strange that this should happen to a narcissus that opens after all the others. I have never known any other daffodil to be defeated by frost but it has happened to my old gardenia daffodil more than once.

4. Primroses

No other flower seems quite so much at home in the cottage garden as does the primrose. It cannot help enjoying itself in that packed, damp atmosphere, with shade from the house or taller plants and plentiful libations of washing-up water and mulchings with tea leaves.

In old gardening books one reads how well the old double primroses grew in cottage gardens, and that is one reason, I think, why we still have them today. They have been cultivated since the first Elizabeth and everyone who has tried to grow them knows that they are not easy to please, so they must have found some peaceful homes to have survived so long. Experts tell us we should divide them regularly—an unnecessary instruction to the greedy ones among us who never have enough—but that is one attention they would not be likely to get in a cottage garden, where plants are usually left to take care of themselves.

There is one famous strain of double primroses that were discovered in the derelict garden of an old cottage. The garden had not been cultivated for at least fifty years, in fact it had returned to meadow turf, and yet young looking plants were regularly found growing there, with double flowers in many pastel shades. I saw some of the plants just as they had been rescued from the wilderness, plants that were almost hidden in the grassy sods in which they were growing.

It remains a mystery how those lovely flowers came to be there, but one theory is that there are some strains of primroses that have a tendency to become double. It sounds too good to be true and I think must be very rare, for all of us who collect double primroses long for the day when we shall find a double among our single flowers. Such a thing did happen to me once. A small double flower appeared in a clump of the low growing deep purple primrose *Primula* × *juliana* 'Jill'. Of course I

31

marked the plant very carefully and each year since I have hope-fully inspected the plant, but there has not been the slightest suspicion of a double since.

I do not think anyone has really discovered the secret of growing double primroses. Some of us are very successful for some years and then for no apparent reason the plants begin to look unhappy and then proceed to die. I do not think there is anything that can be done about it. I have tried cosseting the invalids, potting them in a nice mixture and putting them in a frame, but once they have started down the slippery slope there is no hope for them. The annoying part is that the cause is seldom neglect. It may even be undue fussiness but usually there is no apparent reason.

Some of the healthiest plants I know are in the garden of a small farm in my village. Here they are given all the things we believe they do not want. In the first place they are growing in full sun in a border facing south. The wall of the house is just behind them, so they cannot get much natural moisture. In the normal way they are never divided, although I have been allowed to perform this service when, during the war, I per-suaded the owner to exchange one or two for a priceless half pound of tea! I do not believe they are ever mulched or fed with manure and yet they look marvellously healthy and cover them-selves with little snowy roses every year. They originated, I am told, in a batch of seedlings raised from a packet of mixed seed.

My double white primroses do not behave like that, although they are descendants of the local strain. They have their ups and downs, in spite of all the care I give them. Sometimes I have a flourishing bed of them, at other times they just will not grow well for me. The crowns get hard and knotted, the roots (when I dig them) are short and sparse, and they have none of the exuberant health of my unexpert neighbour's.

The other comparatively easy primrose, *P. vulgaris lilacina fl. pl.*, does far better on the whole. I think I like the double white best but the double lilac is a very close second, and when I see a good clump in full flower I wonder why I bother with all the others. They are all more difficult and really have very little in the way of beauty to put them above the old double lilac, so lovingly called Quakeress, Quaker's Bonnet and Lady's Delight.

The mauvish-red Marie Crousse is usually fairly easy, and I think there are several forms in existence. Marie Crousse to me is more mauve than crimson and the petals have a silver edging. The flowers are usually big and full. Recently another double on the same lines appeared and was called Crousse Plena, but I see no difference between it and the fair Marie. Prince Silverwings is different, with a much more distinct edging in white. The petals are mulberry colour and there is a distinct orange blotch at the base of each with white flecks above.

Mme de Pompadour is another very old one but I do not think anyone considers it easy, and yet I have seen it blooming away quite happily in old gardens where it gets no attention at all. Perhaps that is what it really likes and all my efforts to please are quite unnecessary.

Not many of the coloured primroses we grow today are really old, but there are a few. Miss Massey is one of them. She is said to be the single which gave us Mme de Pompadour, but I find that hard to believe. The Miss Massey I grow is certainly the same colour as Pompadour but there the likeness ends. With me Miss Massey is a much more virile person, with leaves that are extra big and straight, and stand up with great determination. They are much darker in colour than our aristocratic friend, and the flowers that go with them much bigger than the double form.

Bartimeus is the old 'eyeless' primrose, a very dark red with practically no eye (and not very much constitution either!) By sheer meanness I have managed to keep it, it hardly increases at all and seems to have half a foot in the grave most of the time. It gives me much worry because sometimes I think I can see the suspicion of an eye and wonder what has happened, but then we have a good shower of rain and the red velvet turns almost black; it looks as miserable as a newly born black kitten with its little shut eyes, and I know good old Bartimeus is still living with me.

I believe the Caucasian *Primula altaica grandiflora*, sometimes known as *P. amoena*, is an old plant. It is one of the earliest to flower and its delicate pinky-mauve flowers reassure us that spring is on the way. It is a most accommodating little thing and is more tolerant of a rather dry position than many of the primroses.

How long ago Tawny Port left its home in the West of Ireland to be grown in England I do not know but I believe it has been in cultivation for very many years. Very dwarf and very dark, with maroon-green foliage and deep wine flowers, it needs constant care, and I find a top dressing of peat or leaf mould occasionally gives vigour to the little leaves, and they perk up from their horizontal position on the ground. It is definitely a primrose one has to watch if one wants to keep it.

P. × *juliana* Kinlough Beauty is obviously Irish even without the clue of its other name Irish Polly. It looks as though it should be in every cottage garden, with its neat flowers of that shade of bright pink so beloved of cottagers. It has a polyanthus habit and its bright little flowers are neatly divided with white markings round a yellow eye. It is one of the last to flower, and I look forward to its perky little flowers on stiff stems, against a background of flat crinkled leaves. The plants do not exactly run but increase by thick fleshy stems that develop a good root system which can easily be severed if one wants to increase one's stock.

Cottage Maid is not unlike Irish Polly in more subdued colouring and without the sharpness and quartering, not exactly dingy, but perhaps a little blowsy.

There were several old lavender primroses, Duchesse de Parme, Reine des Violettes and Sweet Lavender, but there are very few of them left now. The pink ones are very scarce too, in fact I wonder if they still exist. I had some of them myself, plants such as Rosy Morn, China Rose and Gem of Roses, and the deeper coloured Belle des jardins, but a hot dry summer was too much for them.

I do not think the Garryarde primroses are very old, with their crimson leaves and flowers of pink, magenta or crimson, but I was given one from a cottage garden in Ireland that had blue flowers against leaves with a crimson sheen but with not such a red hue as the Garryardes.

The single green primrose is very old and terribly scarce. It has a poor constitution and needs constant watching. The one with a green foliaceous flower, is far stronger, which is always the way when there is something particularly beautiful. But there is much attraction in the big green flowers on their long stalks and I know if I were sensible I should be grateful for that

and not struggle with its more temperamental shadow. The easy
one has long narrow leaves and the flowers are quite deep in
colour. I remember the late Constance Spry being so smitten
with some I had grown for a flower-arranging group that she
felt she must have some at all costs—and she did.

I must not leave out the Mother of all our coloured primroses,
the little creeping *P. juliae*, with rather small, purple-crimson
flowers, in which the petals are narrow and set rather far apart.
I had its white counterpart once and very lovely it was but it was
too fragile for the jostling life in my garden. I still have a
precious double pink Juliae, which just clings to life in a small
pocket in my ditch garden. It is rather pale and subdued, and I
do not suppose I should fuss over it so much if it were a common
plant.

Some of the polyanthus, or bunched primroses as they used to
be called, are quite old. Princess Charlotte is one of the old
painted polyanthus, a mixture of soft pink, yellow and green—
not exactly glamorous but quite interesting. Prince Albert has
smaller flowers in a deep winy red, laced with silver. The old
Barrowby Gem is one of my favourites, with its pure, pale lemon
flowers, green-eyed and deliciously scented.

The old laced polyanthus are coming back into favour and
great trouble is taken to keep them in cultivation. They are more
interesting than beautiful, with their prim, almost hard little
flowers. I have had Sceptre for many years, with its clear markings in crimson and gold, and another rather tall brown polyanthus with a gold lacing. Coronation is rather flashy with very
bright crimson petals and a broad gold lacing, and Disraeli is also
heavily gold laced.

I like better the polyanthus with silver lacing. The frilly
Arabella is crimson and Rosa Mundi is also crimson and mottled
as well as laced. The crimson ground of Gloriana is very deep in
tone. I have a delightful soft blue polyanthus edged with silver
but have no name for it.

We still have some of the old hose-in-hose primroses although
many have now disappeared. They are not at all easy and I find
it a struggle to keep one or two plants of the pinky mauve Lady
Molly, or Irish Molly as it is sometimes called, and the pink and
cream Lady Lettice. The little candy-striped pink and white is

aptly called The Clown. I think it is an old one and I am sure
that the tall dark red hose-in-hose called Dark Beauty is also old.
I have a dainty little pink hose-in-hose called Flora's Garland and
I used to have a good single pink of the same shade but it has
disappeared; luckily its hose-in-hose form is still with me.

Quite a number of the old named Jacks in the Green have
gone, alas. There was once a Tortoiseshell and a deep sulphur,
Nabob was red and Auburn the tawny shade one would expect,
just as Amber was deep primrose. Feathers has a ruff made of
thin separate sepals. I believe at one time there were varieties
of this 'Jack' with flowers in several colours, but I have never
seen any except the red one, which I still have. The large crimson and gold Salamander, and the squat golden Eldorado still
exist with me, and the pale primrose Orlanda with his outsize
ruff which gets bigger and bigger until it weighs down the
delicate stem. There are still many unnamed 'Jacks' in red and
pink, mauve and white, the deep violet Tipperary Purple and
various polyanthus types.

Not long ago a yellow and green Pantaloon was discovered
in a small garden and was named Greensleeves by the finder. It
has pale yellow flowers and the lower corolla is striped yellow
and green—a combination of hose-in-hose and Jack in the Green
in fact. I also grow a red Pantaloon, with a red and green striped
corolla below the red flower. I enjoy these varieties because they
give me a double flowering. When the plain coloured flower
fades the striped second flower remains attractive for a very long
time and I often wonder if those fascinating heads would grow if
planted in a frame. I have tried to induce the ordinary 'Jacks' to
produce roots, by pegging down the ruffs after the flowers have
finished but they have not shown any disposition to start rooting, so I fear it cannot be done in that way.

5. A Diversity of Plants

It is difficult to know what we mean when we talk about a cottage garden plant. It is usually something that is good-tempered and pleasing, quite an ordinary plant that is not particular about soil or position. Some of them are still listed in a few nurserymen's catalogues, but by degrees they are disappearing and most of us get our odd plants from someone else's garden.

Take, for instance, the tall white daisy once known as *Pyrethrum uliginosum* and now called *Chrysanthemum uliginosum*. Have you ever seen it growing anywhere but in a cottage garden, or listed in a nurseryman's catalogue? I haven't and yet it is a remarkably good plant, with large flowers on tall straight stalks. They are called 'jumpers' by country people because once they start growing they jump up very quickly. *C. uliginosum* hails from Hungary.

I noticed it in two cottage gardens when we first came to this village. In one it was grown in a thick row in front of the cabbages, and there were not many other things in flower at the time. The other planting was even more selective. There is a row of cottages at the end of the village that are built right on the road. The only garden in front is a little strip about two feet wide, between the porches that shelter the front doors, front doors that open right into the sitting-room. A row of *Chrysanthemum uliginosum*, with some pinks in front, grow in front of one of the cottages, and I often wonder why this plant was chosen. I expect it was just given to the owners of the cottage, was planted and has been there ever since.

The ground behind the cottages is about five feet above the level on which they are built, and there is no garden here at all, just a narrow concreted well between the cottage and the high land behind. It always seems dreadful to me that people living in a country village should have no garden round the house, no place

37

for the children to play or to hang the washing, and only allot-
ments down the road in which to grow their vegetables, but the
cottagers do not seem to mind and they plant what they can in
their mean little strips—irises, daffodils, wallflowers and
stocks.

Chrysanthemum uliginosum was a new plant to me, and of
course I felt I could not live unless I got a bit to grow in my own
garden, and I made up my mind to ask for some. I forget now
what I gave in exchange, but I hope it was a generous offering.
I feel very humble when I think of the plants that are given to
me so generously from the smallest gardens, sometimes pieces
of the only plant they have, and which the owners press on me
with such insistence. My garden is very many times the size of
theirs and I have several hundred plants to each one of theirs.

Judging by its name this plant likes to grow in swampy conditions but it does not seem to be very particular about it. It
would probably reach its maximum, seven or eight feet, in a really
damp spot, but that is altogether too tall for most of us and I
prefer the civilised four feet that mine grows. I have never paid
much attention to the plant when once I had got it, but there are
always a few specimens somewhere in the garden. It sows itself
sufficiently to keep the strain going which, I imagine, is the
reason why it has survived so long. It is never a nuisance and
because it is so easy going it gets very little attention from me,
which is base ingratitude on my part. One day I may discover
that it has walked out of my garden. I shall not blame it but will
be very sorry.

There is one plant I know I shall never lose. I often wish I
could and yet I suppose if it did disappear I might be sorry.
Saponaria officinalis is a real cottage garden plant. It was growing in our small front garden when we came here and no doubt
had been there from the days when the house was two cottages.

I cannot remember it in the front garden when we dug out the
dreadful old laurels, levelled the ground and paved it, but it has
been popping up from between the stones ever since. It makes a
thick forest of foliage round the large paving stone outside the
gate, and when it gets really high I tug it out by the roots, because in wet weather anyone who comes into the gate gets
soaked up to the knees. It bears no hard feelings at my brutal

behaviour and in a very few weeks it is all up again and even more luxuriant.

The flowers are really pretty, in a soft pale pink, and most useful for cutting. This is the plant that is used for washing old fabrics and embroideries and I believe has almost miraculous cleansing and brightening properties. I am glad to think it is so good at its own job and fully justifies its name.

The double flowered form is even prettier but quite as determined and I do not wonder that its old name is Bouncing Bet. In my very early gardening days I bought it as 'flos jovis', the description fascinated me and I planted it in one of my terraced beds. Like so many plants that are difficult to eradicate it also takes a long time to establish. But when once it is, it is settled for life and I defy anyone to get rid of it. I have often wondered how far down the roots go. I have dug down several feet and I have never come to the end of the root.

I always associate this plant with the late Mrs Clive of Brympton d'Evercy. It was one of the plants she longed to grow and it simply would not settle down with her. I used to dig down and get up as much root as I could, which she would carry off in triumph, only to come back another day to ask for more. I was as anxious to get rid of it as she was to have it, but however hard we tried neither of us succeeded.

The same thing is now happening to me. Not long ago I was given a small piece of a really deep pink saponaria. I planted it in a place where it could not get up to much mischief if it went away with its usual enthusiasm. But it did not want to grow at all and stayed looking forlorn and miserable until I rescued it and put it in a really very special bed. Now, I suppose, just to spite me, it will start running in all directions among my most cherished treasures and I shall never be able to disentangle it from them.

Campanula glomerata would, I think, be elevated to a most distinguished position in the plant world if it did not run so badly. I do not know how the cottagers manage to control it in their small, thickly planted gardens. Like so many other plants that can be a curse with me it does not appear to be a nuisance with them. I find it almost as difficult to control as saponaria, yet when it flowers I cannot help thinking what a very handsome plant it is. I do not know many flowers in that rich deep blue, and the clustered heads, on stout stems, are most welcome in early summer. I like its country name of Peel of Bells and I also like the white flowered form var. *alba*. White flowers, especially those that do not need staking, are always most useful in the garden.

The violet blue campanula, *C. latiloba*, used to be in every cottage garden, and in many other gardens too for that matter. As a child this was the only campanula I knew and it was the whole family of campanulas to me. For years we hardly saw it, except in tiny gardens, but it has once again come into its own, in a better, deeper form, as C. Highcliffe. I like the old cottage variety when it comes with white flowers, but then I think that any *Campanula latiloba* is worth growing, if only for its foliage. Rather pale in colour, evergreen with long narrow leaves it makes attractive green carpets in sun or shade. It does not run but it increases quite quickly and is an excellent plant for difficult places. I have seen it flowering away happily in the arid soil under a holly tree; it puts itself in walls and delights in covering attractively nasty rubbly corners that can be an eyesore.

I suppose the Pink Cow Parsley, *anthriscus*, was a chance seedling, rescued from the roadside by a humble but keen-eyed gardener. It was doubtless planted tenderly in his little garden and well tended. Pink Lace is not seen in many gardens today which is a pity as it is very easy going and very pretty, and has no bad habits that I know of.

Hieracium aurantiacum is a determined creature. I used to think that the 'grim' in its country name of Grim the Collier came from its inexorable will power to take possession whenever it can, but I discovered in an old book that it is so called because of the black stains at the base of the hairs that cover stem and calyx of the plant. This name is a very old one and I believe comes from a popular comedy of that name in the days of the first Queen Elizabeth. In Buckinghamshire they call it Fox and Cubs, I have heard it referred to as an American Cowslip, and, at times, I have quite another name for it.

There are many places in the garden where one should be grateful for this champion carpeter. Show it a bad corner and it will methodically cover it, ignoring any small plant or weed that happens to be in the way. The bright orange flowers are often welcome in high summer when colour is mostly in blue or pink shades. Our old collier may be rather grim but he is always gay.

I was given a superior form of this Hawkweed with flowers that are rather better in colour, with more red in the orange. In all other respects it is the same, it steamrollers the small fry in just the same way, and is just as easily increased or curtailed. It is very shallow rooting and in my garden has taken a fancy to a paved path where it makes flat carpets on top of the stones.

When the makers of new gardens come to me with big baskets and beg whatever I can spare to cover their bare earth they get solid mats of Grim the Collier with a warning to watch his predatory ways. I often wonder if my warning words are heard and remembered. Probably not, and I have no doubt there are many gardeners who wonder how I ever came to give them such a suspicious character.

The other hieraciums are much safer to introduce. The silver-leafed *H. pilosella* has the same habit of increase as the 'Collier' but is far more modest in the way it goes about it. The beautiful silvery *H. waldsteinii* seeds itself in a mild way, and so does the rather striking *H. praecox*, having green leaves mottled with black.

Cerastium tomentosum is one plant I refuse to give to anybody unless I first get a promise that it will be used exclusively on a wall as far away from any inviting flower bed as possible. I often wonder how the cottage folk manage to control this creeping monster of a plant. But somehow the plants that can become such a menace in a garden like mine seem to behave differently in the tiny packed gardens of the cottagers. It may be that these little gardens are usually so full that there is no room for plants to spread. All the villagers love their Snow-in-Summer and never complain of its wandering ways.

I never fell for cerastium even in my very early, very ignorant days, but I have it in the garden nevertheless. It crept in through the hedge from the cottage next door, and having once got a foothold it proceeded to entrench itself firmly in a place where I could not dislodge it. I dug it out mercilessly from the bed under the hedge but I cannot do anything about a flourishing colony in a paved path nearby. Only poison would make an impression but somehow I cannot bring myself to poison such an artless creature. A wall has now taken the place of the hedge but that will not help me now. The enemy is within the gates and will infiltrate my domain.

I knew one great gardener who said she could never get enough of this whitest of white plants. The late Mrs Clive of Brympton d'Evercy loved to combine crimson and silver and up to her death was working on an ambitious red and silver planting beyond the lake in her garden. I gave her many square yards of the cerastium that kept creeping through the hedge but she always wanted more. Her ambition was to cover the banks of the lake with silver as a foreground to the massed crimsons of trees and shrubs behind. I have no doubt that the busy little cerastium has been carrying on the good work ever since she left off.

6. *Astrantias*

The Masterworts or astrantias are unspectacular plants that belong to the same family as the carrot. They have an old world charm and are often found in cottage gardens. They are difficult to sort out, because forms vary quite considerably, and some of the most interesting variations I know were found in the gardens of cottages in different parts of the country.

Quite indestructible and with pleasant foliage they blend happily with any society in which they find themselves. One old country name is Hattie's Pincushion, and the flowers do look somewhat like pincushions with small umbels surrounded by conspicuous bracts. None of the astrantias are very distinct in colour and that, I suppose, is the reason for another old country name—Melancholy Gentleman. They are not melancholy to me, not even sombre, merely delicate in construction and colour, with a fine upright habit and always smiling faces.

Although there are places in Shropshire (like Stokesay Castle) and Worcestershire where *Astrantia major* has naturalised itself its home is on the Continent, where it grows in many parts of Austria, Switzerland on the edges of woods and in alpine meadows. The tiny *Astrantia minor*, grows in Switzerland and Austria. Other kinds come from Carniola and the Caucasus and a variegated form exists.

Astrantia major is the species most usually grown but it varies in its colouring, some types have more pink, others more green, but all are symphonies of pastel shades and combine off-white, pale green and soft pink.

A very interesting and unusual variation of *Astrantia major* is found in cottage gardens in parts of Gloucestershire. The bracts are pale green, about three times as long as in the normal type, and very shaggy. I have never been able to find any name for this truly decorative flower, nor does it seem to be included in any dictionary. I have been given a plant and I hope it will increase and seed itself as generously as ordinary *Astrantia major* does. I have never discovered if all the Gloucestershire plants came from one chance seedling, or if the plant has a habit of seeding itself in this form when it grows in Gloucestershire.

There are two forms of *Astrantia carniolica*. The more usually grown one has nearly white flowers and nearly white bracts and is, in fact, the most colourless of all the astrantias, and to me it is rather disappointing. But there is a very rare form of *A. carniolica* called *rubra* with flowers of deep rich crimson. Unfortunately, it does not seem quite so tough as the others and is very slow to increase. I am not sure that it does not also sometimes revert to white. It is the last of the astrantias to make its reappearance in the spring and I often get very worried when there is no sign of it, but those bright furled leaves come through in the end. It is one of the ironies of gardening that the unusual, most desirable plants cause much more anxiety and trouble than the ordinary types.

I do not see a great deal of difference between the flowers of *Astrantia biebersteinii* and *Astrantia major*. There may be a little more pink in the former, which comes from the Caucasus, but the variation is very slight. Both grow about eighteen inches to two feet. The leaves, however, are different. In both cases they are five lobed, but in *A. major* the lobes are rounded and in *A. biebersteinii* (and in *A. carniolica* too, for that matter) the lobes are rather long and straight with notched ends.

There is one astrantia that is quite distinct, and that is *Astrantia helleborifolia*, which also comes from the Caucasus. I notice that this species is now called *H. maxima* which is rather confusing when its original name suits it so well. The leaves of this astrantia are three lobed and look just like the leaves of a young hellebore, but in a much lighter, brighter, green. (The leaves of *Helleborus orientalis* are dark green, even in their very early stages, and those of the astrantia are very fresh and shining.)

This is the pinkest of the astrantias, the flowers are pink and the bracts a slightly deeper shade with green on the reverse. But the forms vary. I have found slight variations in plants growing in different gardens and I try if I can to get a fragment of each type so that I can compare them. Even this pink astrantia is not at all showy, the colour is very soft and looks well with almost any other colour—except yellow and orange.

The root system of *Astrantia maxima* is quite different from that of the others. Instead of making separate crowns, which are easily broken apart, this species has running roots and it increases in a more haphazard way. The roots themselves are white and rather fleshy, compared with the hard and woody crowns of the other species. It does not run so much that it is a nuisance. It may start as a small bunch of loose white roots which slowly thicken and expand until all the space around is filled. It has rather the habit of the less invasive campanulas, as, for instance, *C. burghaltii* or *C. carpatica*, and it can be broken up and replanted in the same way.

I often wonder why we all struggle so hard with *Astrantia minor*. I saw it growing first of all in Ireland, a neat little plant with quite small white flowers above the neat mound of foliage. It looked rather like a miniature Fair Maids of France, and just the sort of little plant you would find in a quiet little cottage garden. Having got all the other astrantias, I hankered to possess this one. I tracked it down at Kew but it was a very small and frail little plant that was growing in a little niche in the rock garden. I heard it was also growing in the Cambridge Botanic Gardens and the next time I was there I hunted in vain to find it in the rock garden. Apparently, the scrap of this astrantia had only recently been given to the garden by an enthusiast newly returned from the continent and no one could remember in which cranny in this big new rock garden it had been planted. I was disappointed not to see it but I was secretly rather pleased that even such experts can forget where they plant things. It is something I am always doing myself. I am given a plant I have wanted for ages, I take any amount of trouble to find just the right place for it, and a week later I forget where that place is, and tear round the garden like one demented until I discover where I have put my treasure. A methodical gardener would make notes of when the plant was received and where in the garden it was planted. I always mean to but at the time of planting I feel I could never possibly forget the scene of the ceremonial planting.

The nearest I have got to *Astrantia minor* is sowing seed, which so far has never come up. I ask all my friends who go to Austria and Switzerland to try and find it for me, and I ask all growers of unusual plants if they have it. And, if I ever get it, I wonder if I shall succeed in pleasing it? In his book about his garden in Gloucestershire the late Canon Ellacombe bemoans the fact that it is such a little beast, although he is much too polite to put it quite like that. Mr Bowles realised it was difficult for in his book 'My Garden in Spring' he says that to his surprise it has settled down.

The present interest in astrantias is just another example of the uncanny way the cottagers had of finding and keeping a good plant. These flowers have been grown for many years in cottage gardens, and they looked perfectly at home there. Now other people are discovering how beautiful they are and the nurseries cannot keep up with the demand. They fit in so well with our informal mixed borders and are the perfect plants to grow with shrubs; they are, in fact, the best of good mixers.

7. The Old Pinks

Whenever we think of an old world garden we think of pinks. Gillyflowers, they were called in the old days, or Sweet Johns, and they belong, more than any other flower, to the days of sun bonnets and print gowns and the little crowded gardens of the past.

There are certain old pinks that are easy going and very fragrant which are always referred to as 'cottage pinks'. What exactly constitutes a cottage pink I do not know, and I think it must be an embracive term for any good-tempered, sweet smelling pink that has not a definite name. A garden I know well has a border of 'cottage' pinks in front of roses. They are small and double and the colour is that ordinary, slightly mauve pink that was so popular last century. The pinks grow on stiff stalks about 9 to 10 in tall which makes them very useful for picking. They are extremely strong and healthy and go on year after year without any attention.

Old laced pinks and Painted Ladies are cottage pinks too. The colliers of Durham and Northumberland were great growers of pinks, and that tight little band of craftsmen near Glasgow, the Paisley weavers, made the cult of laced pinks a substitute for worldly delights. They are said to have had between seventy and eighty different ones in regular cultivation.

In the pinks that were largely grown in cottage gardens, scent was more important than shape or colour. The old Crimson Clove, which surely has the best scent of all, is seldom seen now except in the old gardens, and Mrs Sinkins, with her rather untidy habit, has been superseded by newer varieties that are neater and more shapely, but they have not the heavenly scent of Mrs Sinkins, who is still treated with respect in small country gardens.

I wonder if the old crimson Sops in Wine is still being

cherished in some old garden. It must have had a very strong scent to be used in the making of mulled wine. The Fenbow, or Nutmeg Clove, has rather small deep crimson flowers and is strongly scented. It seems to have a strong constitution, as I have discovered. I was given a small plant and as I knew it was a real treasure I planted it in a trough near my garden door, where I could check on it many times a day and be quite sure it was well and happy. I ought to have known better than to plant it in a trough filled, for the most part, with peat. Other small pinks that I planted in the same place—the brilliant single scarlet Holbein pink and the most temperamental Napoleon III— showed their disgust for such soft living by fading away after they had flowered. But the old Fenbow Clove paid no attention to the soil he was in and gets bigger and stronger every year. I keep him in check by removing a large number of cuttings each year. I wonder how enormous he would get if I put him in a cranny between stones which is where, of course, he ought to be.

Many people today are collecting old pinks and endeavours are being made to find as many of the old ones as possible. Bridal Veil is one of them. As one would naturally assume it is white, but white with a greenish centre and a light crimson patch at the base of the petals. It is fringed and strongly scented.

The Montrose pink, now called Cockenzie, is a neat little flower in double red with a centre so dark that it is almost purple. I grew it many years ago and I am ashamed that I have not got it now. It dates from about 1720 so it is a plant worth chasing and cherishing when once it is run to earth.

Another old one is Dad's Favourite, in double white heavily laced with chocolate and with a dark centre. The Chelsea pink, dated about 1760, is also known as Little Old Lady. It is small and double in bright crimson, laced with white.

Fringed pinks are typical of the cottage garden, the old white or pink, and some named varieties, which are still being culti- vated today. Fimbriata is a large ivory, the Earl of Essex is double rose-pink with a small dark eye, and Sam Barlow is a large double white with an almost black centre. The bright salmon single fringed pink which is now called Day Dawn is, I think, the same as the old Earl of Carrick. It is a beautiful plant but not the easiest to keep. I spend my days trying to make it happy but it has not really settled down with me and I am constantly realising that it has walked out on me again, and I have to go round begging from my friends.

Some of the old pinks may seem rather blowsy by our standards. Glory is a very large, rather untidy double in deep rose, laced and zoned with maroon. Its wonderful scent makes up for its lack of shapeliness. Rose de Mai is little better in the way of shape but its colour is more refined, a really good pink, without any trace of mauve. I grow an interesting little double pink called Ruffling Robin. It is rather dumpy but its pink is very bright and clear and it is heavily stippled with maroon. It came from an old garden and seems to have a strong constitution.

From another old garden I was given two neat little pinks, one single and the other double. The single one is called Argus and it is nearly always in bloom. It is white with a deep maroon centre, and the other, which is double and is called Pheasant's Ear, is also white and maroon.

For many years I have grown a very handsome bright crimson pink, with white markings. It has long stiff stalks and everyone who sees it wants a cutting. It was given to me by the late Mrs Clive of Brympton d'Evercy, and to identify it I called it Brympton Red. I have since learned that it came in the first place from the garden of the workhouse in Beaminster. Another old friend was given cuttings many years ago and it was she who passed it on to Mrs Clive.

I wonder if gardeners who have Inchmery in their gardens realise that it is a very old pink. It is quite small and in a wonderful shade of silvery pink. It came to me from a cottage garden but I notice it is mentioned in several old gardening books. Two others that are still being cultivated and which are also referred to very often are Donizetti, a single red with a dark eye, and Ruth Fischer, very small and very white, with dark buds and particularly good foliage.

There must have been a grower of pinks named Bat, as well as that famous and often mentioned fancier, Master Tuggie. Bat's Double Red is still being grown and is worthy of preservation. It is rather small and neat and a good doer. It is a miracle that Caesar's Mantle and Wm Brownhill are still in existence as they are both very difficult to propagate. Caesar's Mantle is crimson, with a dark centre, and Wm Brownhill white with maroon markings so dark that they are almost black. This old pink is particularly well shaped in a precise, classical way. I have read about another very famous old pink but I have never seen it and I do not know if it even exists today, but I hope it is tucked away in some little old garden somewhere. St Phocas's Nosegay is said to have fringed petals with purplish markings on a light crimson ground.

Mule pinks always seem to me to be typical cottage garden flowers, with their green leaves and heads of rather small double flowers. I wonder if other gardeners are as ignorant as I was and talk glibly about 'mule' pinks without realising the significance of the name.

I believe the mule pink originated from a deliberate cross between a carnation and a Sweet William early in the eighteenth century, and was then christened a 'mule' pink. They are sterile, like their bad tempered four-legged namesakes, and some of them try so hard to flower themselves to death that it is really astounding they are still in existence today. It says a lot for the perseverance of some of the old growers.

Some of them, of course, are not difficult to keep. *Dianthus carthusianorum* v. *multiflorus* is the bread and butter member of the family, easy, long-lived and only too willing to oblige with plenty of cuttings. I have had a plant in my garden for over twenty years. I always mean to propagate it, in case I wake up one day and find it gone, but I never do. It is growing in a most awkward place, in the shade of a myrtle that has grown into a very big bush since the pink was planted, and which now shades it completely. The beautiful salmon pink Emil Paré is not nearly so self-effacing. If it does not get plenty of attention it removes itself to another sphere, and I have had to start again several times. It sometimes reverts to its magenta-ish parent. Not only do flowers in the two colours appear on the same plant, but sometimes the individual flowers have splashes of deep magenta on their petals. There is another shell-pink 'mule' being cultivated today called Salmonea, but wherein lies the difference I do not know, but I shall compare them closely when both are in flower. People who grow the newcomer say that it is an improved form of Emil Paré, and is scented. I have never noticed any scent from Emil Paré so perhaps that is the difference.

The oldest mule pink we know today is Napoleon III, a small bright crimson that has the tiresome habit of flowering itself to death. It does not have a very strong constitution to begin with and its leaves are very wispy and a pale yellow green compared with the strong fresh green of *multiflorus* and Emil Paré. Not long ago a new mule pink made its appearance, called Casser's Pink. I do not know its history but I do know that it is not Napoleon III as some people have suggested. It is very bright and gay and flowers very well, but I have heard complaints that it is not completely hardy and can be killed by an exceptionally cold winter.

The only way that I know to keep Napoleon III going is to snatch a few cuttings very early in the season before he has begun to think about flowering. That is the only chance, for to leave it a little later is to find that the plant is all flower buds and no cuttings. Proud owners of several plants can sacrifice one plant for the good of posterity. As soon as a bud starts to form it is nipped off without ceremony, and the plant will then provide plenty of cuttings.

There used to be a white form of Napoleon III called Marie Paré, but I have never seen it. It may be lurking somewhere and I never give up hope of finding it some day. It is said to be as difficult to keep as Napoleon III, so it is not surprising that it has gone from us.

Another white mule pink, *Dianthus fragrans*, does not appear to be grown any longer either. It had small fringed white flowers slightly splashed with purple. It was sweetly scented with a perfume reminiscent of jasmine. The double form sounds even more alluring with flowers the size of a silver threepenny piece.

I still struggle with the single bright scarlet-red dianthus, *D.* × *atkinsonii*, surely the most outstanding of all the mules. The rather large single red flowers are of the most intense red and they are borne on slender stalks about a foot in height. It is said to be a chance hybrid seedling of *D. chinensis*, the Chinese or Indian pink, and is, alas, sterile. To keep it is even more of a feat than to cling to Napoleon III, and again it is recommended to keep one plant for cuttings, but first find your plant. Fortunately cuttings root easily. I take every scrap of green that I can safely remove from my one plant when it is not looking and they usually strike. The parent plant always passes away after flowering so cuttings are one's only hope.

The fringed white, very sweet scented *Dianthus superbus* of Europe and Asia is regarded as one of the species from which many of our garden pinks are descended. It is very old, even mentioned in Parkinson, but I do not know anyone who has it today.

Another mule pink that seems to have disappeared from nurserymen's lists, and I fear from cultivation, is a double rose mule called Fettes Mount. We know it is Scottish in origin and one still hopes to find it one day somewhere, with some of the other old pinks that made the little gardens so gay in the old days.

One occasionally sees the bigger flowered pinks, which I suppose should rightly be called carnations, but they are not grown in the way carnations are usually cultivated, which means disbudding and very careful staking. In the cottage garden all the buds are allowed to flower. I have a very old plant which I believe is called Reine Hortense. The flowers are a very pale, delicate pink, and they come when all the other dianthus have finished flowering. There are so many buds that it is difficult to pick a flower without sacrificing a few and I often wonder if I should be brutal and remove some. It has the peculiarity of occasionally producing flowers that are splashed with vivid red.

Marie Antoinette has somewhat the same habit but the flowers are bigger and there are not so many of them. The colour is a deep rich pink, with no trace of mauve. Rifleman, as one would assume, is a vivid scarlet and makes a very bright patch in the garden. The Old Clove pink was the best of the lot but it is difficult to find the free flowering strain that was the joy of every cottage garden. I have been given several forms but none of them is as generous or as strongly scented as the one's I remember in my Mother's garden.

8. *Wall Gardening*

One reason why the plants in cottage gardens look so very happy is, I think, because the little gardens are usually enclosed, sometimes with hedges but very often with walls.

As one would expect the walls are nearly always old and crumbling—an ideal place for all the little plants that love to seed themselves in the inviting crevices. And once there they are left in peace to enjoy a long life and to scatter their progeny in other crannies in the old wall.

We have almost forgotten that wallflowers are so named because they are at home in a wall. We are so used to seeing them treated as biennials and bedded out each year with mathematical precision, that those which appear in walls are treated as weeds. I have a very old wall that screens me from the road. It is almost too full of gaps for safety but it is a perfect paradise for plants that like to grow in a wall. I have not grown wallflowers deliberately for many years but when I did, nearly twenty years ago, it was to fill up odd gaps in the borders and not to plant in a bed by themselves. The ones I grew were usually such strains as the delicate flame pink Eastern Queen, the pale Primrose Monarch and the rich Ruby Gem. Where, then, did the strangers in my wall come from? They live there, year after year, a bright yellow and the typical cottage tawny-brown, which glows in the sunshine. No latter day named variety can produce anything like the strong, sweet scent of those dessicated veterans that sun themselves in the wall year after year. One wonders how any nourishment can be extracted from the old mortar but the flowers are large and glow with health.

Snapdragons—I am sure our friends in the cottages never called them antirrhinums—love to grow in walls too, and when they get a good foothold they hang on from year to year and establish their perennial inheritance. The colours, as a rule, are deep burgundy or a rather strident pink. Then there are the old striped antirrhinums, which are still being grown today. A favourite striped variety was Hendersoni, with large flowers on a medium stalk. A good many named varieties were grown in the old days, and some of their children may have survived to this day.

White arabis (*A. albida*) loves to sow itself in an old wall and from a tiny crevice will make great mats of foliage that hang down for a foot or more. That was one plant I found growing in our walls when we came here and which is still with me. The villagers call it Snow-on-the-Mountain and esteem it highly. I am afraid I treat it more drastically than they would, cutting it right back to the wall every summer. It then produces strong new foliage and is very pleasant for the rest of the year.

Snow-in-Summer is, of course, *Cerastium tomeniosum* and is even more highly prized than white arabis. What surprises me is that it never appears to become a nuisance in a cottage garden. I am sure it is not discouraged in the rude way in which I snub it, and yet one does not see cottage walls smothered under its delicate embrace.

Golden alyssum(*A. saxatile*) is a great favourite for the old walls. The villagers name it Gold Dust and it is one of the favourite village flowers. I would not let my village friends know that I find it a little overpowering and do my best to grow the gentle lemon-coloured var. *citrinum* instead. I do not succeed, of course. The little plants of lemon-coloured alyssum that I put in year after year either disappear or change colour, because every spring without fail the garden is again full of great roaring splashes of hot, hard yellow. If one of my plants of the pale alyssum manages to survive it is always a frail and sickly creature beside its bouncing relation.

There is no plant quite so good for growing in a wall as valerian in red, or pink or white. Why the villagers should call it Kiss-me-Quick I have never discovered. Another old name is Pretty Betsy and there is a legend that the Pied Piper used a concoction made from the roots of valerian to lure his rats. The most spectacular display of valerian that I know is on a cottage wall near me. It is all the same shade, the best shade, a rich crimson. I cannot think how it is done. I try my hardest to concentrate on this colour on my walls. I cut off all the finished flowers on plants of white and pale pink and leave the crimson to seed as hard as it likes. I rescue and replant the seedlings that appear round the best shades of red, but I always have far more of the ugly wishy-washy pink. A certain amount of pink makes a pleasant variation but the pinks vary and there are many shades more attractive than the pale mauve-pink which seems to like me best. White valerian, used in moderation, is very attractive, but none of the others come up to the glowing crimson as I admire it on that humble cottage wall.

There will nearly always be Yellow Stonecrop (*Sedum acre*) covering flat surfaces of the old walls, that industrious little stonecrop that goes by the name of wall pepper because the leaves have a peppery taste. It is a British native but that does not stop it from being a cherished wall plant in the humbler gardens.

Creeping Jenny (*Lysimachia nummularia*) is a British native too but it likes to get into a garden with its betters. It seems strange that this industrious little plant that chooses a damp place when it can is quite at home on the shady side of a wall. The golden leaved form is wonderful for brightening up a dark corner. I always think these plants are worthy of a better appreciation than they usually have, and they get it in the cottage gardens.

Nothing could keep the yellow corydalis out, nor erinus if there is any growing nearby to produce the seeds. The commonest erinus is *E. alpinus* and I have seen it smothering ugly ruins with its little mauve flowers. I have had it several times but I cannot keep it any more than I can keep the beautiful pink variety Mrs Charles Boyle, with its bigger flowers. The one that does best for me is the magenta-purple Dr Hanelle. Years ago I bought a plant and now it has sown itself in both sides of a wall in my garden. Individually the flowers are small but there are so many of them that the wall positively glows when the erinus is in bloom. In another part of the garden I have one or two plants of the white form. I do not know how I got them in the beginning and I always wonder how long I shall keep them for they do not seed themselves like the others.

I expect the white erinus was a chance seedling for in the

same way there will sometimes appear little plants of *Oxalis floribunda* in white as well as pink in the old cottage walls. The usual place for 'Shamrock', as the villagers call it, is in old stone troughs or poking through the railings at the roadside but it will sometimes sow itself in a wall crevice. An ideal place is on top of the wall as it needs the sun if it is to open its gay pink flowers. This modest little plant was one of the first things I noticed when we first came to Somerset, sunning itself in little gardens. In a nearby village the houses are built high above the road, in fact it seems typical of Somerset to have roads cut out so that fields, orchards and cottages are high above the road. This means that there are many walls and it was on top of these and in the narrow strips of gardens that I first noticed the pink oxalis, which blooms from early spring till late autumn, and only asks for the sun to shine.

The charm of the old walls is the glorious mixture of all kinds of plants. There is no snobbery, the cobweb sempervivum (*S. arachnoideum*) may hobnob with the humble Ivy-leaved Toad-flax (*Cymbalaria muralis*). An aristocratic saxifrage such as *S. longifolia* may have lodged in a crevice when it was very small and then find itself with the irrepressible native Pennywort, *Umbilicus rupestris*, as a neighbour. It is an attractive plant with its round shining leaves which look as though they had been made of green wax. The country name for it is Penny Pies and it likes to find sanctuary in a crumbling wall, where it will not be disturbed.

We usually grow our pinks in an ordinary flower bed but their natural way of growing is between stones or on a rocky hillside. If pinks were more generous with their seed we should see many of them in old walls. I am always meaning to plant small cuttings of *Dianthus gratianopolitanus* (*syn. D. caesius*), the Cheddar Pink, and seedlings of the Maiden Pink, *Dianthus deltoides*, in wall crevices and see how they get on.

Thrifts, mossy saxifrages and alpine strawberries all seed themselves in wall crevices. The little rock campanulas, *C. portenschlagiana* and *poscharskyana*, manage to insinuate themselves into every part of the garden, and they are most effective in walls. The little pink and white daisies of *Erigeron mucronatus* of Mexico bloom all through the year, and no one minds how many new seedlings appear each year. The little pink daisy known as Felicity (one time *Felicia petiolata*) was growing in a cottage garden near me and I was given a seedling. Now I have to be very firm with it. Its proper name is *Aster petiolatus* and it likes to climb instead of descending. Put it at the bottom of a wall and it will grow straight up, anchoring itself in convenient crevices as it goes, and sowing its seed above its head.

It always amazes me to see *Campanula pyramidalis*, the Chimney Bell flower, towering out of a wall but that is where it likes to put itself, so do foxgloves and verbascums and I have even seen the big yellow *Achillea filipendulina* growing out of a wall. So there is no monotony and these giants are a happy contrast to the little ferns that love to grow in old walls. The ferns most usually grown are the rusty-back fern (*Ceterach officinarum*), Common Spleenwort or Maidenhair Spleenwort (*Asplenium trichomanes*) and Wall-Rue (*Asplenium ruta-muraria*). Sometimes aquilegias put themselves in a wall, *Fuchsia gracilipes* often does, and occasionally there will be a flourishing wild rose growing in the wall. I found a wild rose in one of my walls when we came here and I tried to bud a China rose on to it but I was not successful!

9. *Auriculas*

Auriculas (*Primula auricula*), or Bear's Ears, because of their pointed leaves, are among the oldest plants we grow. Gerard mentions them in his Herball published in 1597. He calls them Mountain Cowslips and from his description it is obvious that the one he is referring to is the yellow alpine auricula.

Many of the most interesting auriculas came to this country with the Flemish weavers about 1575. These craftsmen settled in different parts of the country, notably Ipswich, Norwich and Rochdale, and afterwards miners in Lancashire and Cheshire took up the craze and spent sums out of all proportion to their wages to buy new and unusual varieties.

They grew striped auriculas and double auriculas, and of course the edged auriculas, which have been developed to such a state of perfection today. Some of the expensive and difficult plants they grew were no doubt the 'show' or 'stage' varieties, with their powdered faces and mealy leaves. There is no mention in old records that they were grown outside. They do not mind cold, of course, but rain plays havoc with the delicate powdered surface of the flowers and leaves, and for the most part they were grown in frames. Theatres were even built to show off their charms and the pampered pets were staged with infinite care and much artistry. The weavers, for the most part, worked at home, and they did not mind working late at night to make up for the time taken off during the day to move the auriculas from place to place during the heat of the day. If the frames could not be adequately shaded they would be hidden in a dark corner to avoid the glare of the sun. Heat in itself does not bother them but direct sunlight at flowering time does.

Infinite trouble was taken in the growing of these plants and the most elaborate composts were concocted to please them, with such strange ingredients as blood from the butcher, yeast

58

scum from the baker, sand from the sea shore, various types of manure and loam from a wheat field.

The auriculas that have survived in our cottage gardens were not pampered like this. They had to make the best of whatever corner they were given, it might be in full sun or a dank and sunless strip beneath a wall.

Occasionally a show auricula came into the possession of a humble gardener and by some miracle it survived. I was given a piece of a very old auricula called the Duke of Edinburgh, that came from an old cottage garden. The leaves were so powdered that they were nearly white and the flowers were a soft brick red, like the faded hangings in an ancestral home. It did very well for me for several years but one sad morning in a dry summer I found it had severed all connection with its roots, and though I hopefully put what was left in a frame it did not have the heart to try all over again. I cannot forgive myself for this callousness, but with a big garden and so many treasures to cherish it is quite impossible to take care of everything in a drought. I rush round every waking hour with a watering pot and haul the hose from place to place from early morn till dusk descends, but something inevitably gets overlooked. I wish it could have been something less precious than the old Duke of Edinburgh.

Another old plant disappeared at about the same time. It was a double brown auricula that was found in a cottage garden in Crewkerne, just a few miles from me. I did not get it from Crewkerne as it had to go all the way to Scotland to an auricula specialist before I came to hear of it. I still have a double pink variety, which is more interesting than beautiful. 'Pink' is a flattering term to use for the rather dirty nondescript colour, but it is nearer pink than anything else, and it is certainly double.

The auriculas usually grown in cottage gardens are the dark velvety purples and blues. Old Irish Blue with its frilled petals and white eye is one of the most attractive. Crimson-black is another old cottage plant with flowers of the darkest velvety-red. I used to have Blue Velvet, rather small and neat, and with a white eye, but somehow it did not survive in spite of all my love and care.

Probably it is the Old Dusty Miller that one associates chiefly with cottage gardens. Though they are powdered, and one might well feel they should be treated as show varieties, they are, in fact, remarkably tough and need no special treatment. The one most usually grown is the Old Yellow Dusty Miller. It is a lovely thing with its soft yellow flower and white, powdered leaves. The Old Red Dusty Miller varies in shade in different places, but usually it is a rich claret. Then there is the Old Purple Dusty Miller which is a most typical cottage garden plant.

How one should grow auriculas I really do not know. There does not seem to be any fixed rule. I have seen them flowering magnificently in full sun and not blinking an eyelid when the sun shines right into their eyes, which is quite contrary to the maxims of the old growers. Then I have admired them flowering just as well without any sun at all. Like so many other flowers I think they do best for the people who do not fuss over them too much. I have planted mine in half a dozen different positions, in shade and sun, in rock crevices on a steep bank and in rock garden crannies. They have been given super soil in a stone trough and leafmould on a woodland bank but I cannot say I am really proud of any of them. Old Irish Blue on a raised bank and growing near stones is doing as well as any. The double pink in peat in a trough increases slowly and flowers well, and the old double brown, which I wedged so carefully so that it had shade from stones above, did not last very long. I have had pale misty-blue auriculas, velvety browns, primrose yellows and rose madders but I do not have them now. I feel sure that if I just put them in some odd corner and forgot about them they would grow and flower well for me as they do in the little cottage gardens, and I would be able to pull them to pieces and replant the nicely rooting little sections in a mixture of sand and peat.

10. Fumitory

One of the prettiest little plants that grows in every cottage wall is *Corydalis lutea*. This plant has so many things to recommend it that I can never understand why we do not treat it better. Instead of hounding it out of our gardens (or trying to, for nothing in this world could oust it altogether) we should really be grateful for its beauty. Its delicate blue-grey foliage is finely cut and exquisite in every detail. There are not many evergreen plants with half its charm nor its generosity. Just as the leaves are the same, summer and winter, so are the flowers. It never stops flowering and the little yellow flowers are worth examining closely, like so many of our flowers which we seldom take the trouble to study.

The cottagers call this corydalis Wee Folks' Stockings and I am sure never treat it as brutally as I do, tearing it from my walls and digging it out with a knife from its niche among the stems of a favourite fuchsia. I do not think the little plants would do any harm if I let them grow wherever they wanted, those transparent and brittle stems could not hurt anyone, but it is like some very quiet and gentle people, extremely persistent, and it tries to take possession of my garden.

I have now started to grow a white flowered form and I wonder if it will in time become a nuisance too? At the moment I feel I should not mind because I am enchanted by its purity and grace, and it has inspired me to work even harder to eradicate its less appealing little sister.

Indiscriminate seeding seems a habit of the corydalis. To my knowledge I did not introduce the ferny-leaved *C. cheilanthifolia* into the garden. It appeared in a crevice between stones on my ditch bank. I had never seen it before and thought it was a weed. To begin with I pulled out the plants that kept appearing in odd places, and then it dawned on me that even if they were weeds

61

they were extremely beautiful ones and well worth growing in any place where ferny foliage would be an asset. Now I have a flourishing colony in a pocket in the ditch and could make several more if I replanted the myriads of seedlings that pop up all round. The leaves have a certain amount of bronze in the green and they look very much like the fronds of the Lip-fern. The flowers are yellowish but there is some green and brown in them too so that they blend very happily with their leaves. It is a Chinese plant and I should much like to know how it got into my garden.

I know how another ferny-leaved corydalis came to live with me. I saw it seeding itself in the paving of a friend's garden and was given some microscopic seedlings, which I wrapped in a hand-kerchief for safety. Now it is doing the same for me in my small paved garden. It is, I feel sure, just another form of *C. cheilanthifolia* with more colour in the leaves. Another friend has one which is much deeper in colour, almost bronze, and grown singly with a good background it is singularly effective.

All the members of the family have the same spurred type of flower. The name comes from the Greek *korydalis*, a crested lark, and according to Mr Bowles it is the bird's hind toe-nail that the spur on the flowers resembles.

There is another evergreen corydalis, an aristocrat this time, the blue-leaved *C. wilsonii*. It is rather a flat little plant, which does best in a sunny position in rather light soil. The leaves spread themselves to make a delicate pattern against the ground, and the lemon-coloured flowers are gently touched with green.

I wish the other members of the family kept their leaves. I am always fearful for the plants that disappear completely after flowering for they are liable to be disturbed unless one's garden is absolutely bristling with labels. I am always looking for places in which to put new plants and though I ought to know by now that if there is a patch of bare soil visible it is because the occupant has got his head under the counter, it does not stop me from poking in something else.

But it takes a lot to oust a corydalis completely. When I have realised that I have planted one of the family in the wrong place and removed it elsewhere I always find a few leaves coming up each year in the old place, like the wreckage above a sunken ship.

This can be very useful sometimes. I have the regrettable habit of removing my plants from one part of the garden and putting them in another place where I think they would be happier, or look nicer, and then forgetting where they have finally been settled. *C. solida* has been moved about quite a bit but I never get up quite all the little bulbs, which is probably why I still have it after twenty years.

I was given it in the first place by a cottager in the village. His little front garden was full of it and I often wondered how it first got there.

When we came to the village the cottage had a porch covered with Winter Jasmine and was called Jasmine Cottage. The windows were very small and crowded with plants, and the rooms had low ceilings and high settles. The old lady who lived there followed the local home industry of gloving, helped by her deaf and dumb daughter.

I well remember the consternation when, for some reason unknown, the jasmine over the porch died, and the long discussions that followed as to whether the name of the cottage would have to be changed!

The old beams are still in the cottage but the little old windows have been changed to bigger ones. There is light paint and modern furniture and the garden has been completely remade with tea roses and polyanthus. But in spite of all the excavating and remaking a few small tufts of *Corydalis solida* come up every year.

I think this corydalis when it really settles down, must seed itself nearly as persistently as *C. lutea*. Anyone who has visited the garden of St John's College Oxford in March and April will have noticed how *Corydalis solida* has taken possession of the beds under the trees and shrubs. There must be hundreds and hundreds of these loose lavender flower heads growing among the trees and I make a yearly pilgrimage to see them whenever I can.

Corydalis cava is so-called because of its hollow bulb. Its flowers are of pale lilac, not unlike those of solida, but tighter and more fleshy. The leaves are rather fleshy too, in fact I think it could more rightly be called solida than the airy-fairy plant that bears that name. There is a white flowered form, but to me both somehow miss the quality that would make them first class plants. They grow rather floppily and untidily and they are not nearly so satisfactory in the garden as *C. solida*. This corydalis makes an erect, compact clump which shows to advantage its closely clustered rosy-purple flowers. It always reminds me of a little group of people standing back to back. I always have liked people to hold themselves well and keep their heads up as if they were proud to face the world, and this is just what *C. solida* does.

Corydalis nobilis comes from Siberia and I had no idea before I made the acquaintance of this charmer that Siberia could produce anything so pleasant. I think it is well named because it really is a lovely, noble plant with an enchanting blackish-green tip to each canary-coloured flower, which is as bewitching as a human dimple. It flowers in May, when it has the scene to itself.

What does one say about *Corydalis cashmeriana* except that it is unbelievably lovely, rather expensive and highly temperamental. The blue of its flowers is as deep and penetrating a blue as I know. It looks right through you and then, having established relations, it decides it does not like you much after all and goes off to its plant heaven. I have yet to meet the gardener who grows this plant so well that he can tell me how he does it, but I shall try again in another part of the garden and go on trying until in the end I win over the unapproachable beauty.

Phlox, lupins and
cornflowers are
among the flowers
that fill the garden
of this Wiltshire
cottage.

Another cottage in
Wiltshire with
hydrangeas and
shasta daisies.
Thrift and pinks are
growing at the edge
of the path.

Stone steps lead to a flagged path, edged with box. Clipped bushes and brick path add old-world charm.

A rose covered arch and standard rose trees are packed behind this cottage hedge, with a shaped yew by the gate.

Left: Cottage gardening at its best, with bold clumps of geraniums and campanula, stocks and ivy against a background of shrubs.

Right: Madonna lilies seem to do far better in a cottage garden than anywhere else. They enjoy the shade and freedom from disturbance.

Left: Thatched cottages at Ebbesbourne Wake in Wilts., with little gardens against the road. *Right:* Another delightful cottage garden in the same village. Old straddle stones and sloping lawn are in keeping with the cottage.

Under the shade of old apple trees simple flowers grow in gay profusion, with hedge behind and flower decked porch.

Ferns, hedges and shaped yews against stone paving make a garden that is furnished and attractive all through the year.

Hollyhocks are true cottage garden flowers and here they are lovely against the whitewashed walls of a thatched cottage.

Creepers smother the porch and cover the walls of this old cottage. Pinks and roses fill the garden.

Left: Dicentra spectabilis, the old Bleeding Heart, is seen in cottage gardens more than anywhere else. *Right: Astrantia major,* sometimes called Hattie's Pincushion or the Melancholy Gentleman.

A row of red or yellow Crown Imperials is a typical feature of cottage gardens.

The cottage is reached under rose covered arches with daffodils at their base, and low growing plants over the path.

Roses frame leaded windows and big clumps of lavender and rosemary spread over the brick path of an Ardingly cottage.

Well-covered walls,
a tiny lawn and
beds packed with
flowers make this
corner cottage in
Lacock a pleasant
spot.

This neat cottage
in Lindfield has
old-fashioned
flowers surrounding
a brick path.

Left: Dad's Favourite is an old double pink. *Right:* Double Sweet Rocket used to grow in cottage gardens but is difficult to find today.

Left: Sticky Nellie (*Lychnis viscaria flore-pleno*) has brilliant magenta-pink flowers on long sticky stalks. *Right:* Cottagers love *Cerastium tomentosum* which they call Snow-in-Summer and grow on their walls.

Pinks and phlox are among the flowers that fill these cottage gardens in Melksham, Wilts., with climbers framing the doorways.

A typical cottage medley with gladioli grown in a long row, and stone edges to the beds.

Apples and tomatoes are among the flowers in a packed garden at
Bowden Hill, Lacock. The dahlias are lovingly staked.

Tobacco plants and other annuals help to make this display at
Batsford, Herts., where the cottagers vie with each other.

Mind your own Business (*Helxine solierolii*) used to be a favourite cottage window pot plant.

London Pride (*Saxifraga umbrosa*) makes itself at home anywhere and loves the shade of cottage gardens.

The full double blooms of *Peony officinalis* in pink, white or red last for weeks.

Raised borders,
well filled with
plants have the
added attraction of
steps and a rose
covered arch.

Roses frame the
windows of an
Ardingly cottage.
Lavender grows
beside a brick path
with a golden
conifer opposite.

A cottage in a woodland setting has very tightly crammed flower beds with roses and tall, towering delphiniums.

Clumps of lavender beside a stone path and tall hollyhocks rising above the well-kept hedge in the background.

A generous mixture of cottage flowers are packed behind the wall that makes the corner of a village in Balcombe.

Hollyhocks are a feature of this cottage at Brockham Green, with a big bush of rosemary and handsome conifers.

11. Daisies

No self-respecting cottage garden would be without its little edging of daisies. Rather prim and always well behaved nothing could fit in better with the narrow paths and edgings of shells or bricks. Daisies prefer a moist situation so grow well beneath the dripping eaves and make gay little borders at the bottom of the cottage walls or peeping through the fence against the road.

The old name for daisy was, Day's Eye, because the flowers open with the dawn. That is the ordinary daisy, *Bellis perennis*, that studs our lawns and inspired Robert Burns to write his poem apologising for having to cut off the head of the 'wee crimson-tipped flower'. The flowers close at night and will also shut up during the day if the weather is dull or rainy to protect the pollen. It is from this modest little plant that our cultivated daises are descended. They are among the oldest of our flowers, for Parkinson both illustrated and described them in his Paradisus ed. i, 1629. From time immemorial country children have made daisy chains, and that custom has survived, although others, like the making of cowslip balls, have died out.

Alas, many of the old daisies have disappeared from cultivation, judging by the lists that are given in old gardening books. I should like to be able to grow one called The Bride, with white flowers as large as a crown piece and its pink and rose companion most properly called The Bridegroom. Where I wonder is that strong purplish-pink daisy called Eliza or the carmine Glory of Frankfurt, which produced flowers on exceptionally long stalks. There were Rubens in crimson-scarlet, the mottled Crown, Rose Conspicua and Venus, Snowflake and Snowball all, of course, white. Some of these may be included in the mixtures we grow from seed, but I do not believe anyone grows them by name any more.

There are, however, many named daisies still being cultivated, some of the cottage gardeners grow them, others prefer
the bigger double forms of *Bellis perennis*, which make more
show.

I do not know when the dainty little Dresden China daisy
first made its appearance. It is the same size and habit as our
little native daisy but its double flowers are a ravishing shade of
pink. It is well named, I always think, because it is one of the
most delicate and charming little plants one can have but it is
definitely not a plant that can be planted and forgotten. It needs
dividing very regularly and it hates to dry out. I find it does
best in moist crevices between paving stones or grown tight
against the edge of a stone path. In each case the roots are kept
cool and moist. It can disappear very easily and I am always
meeting gardeners who say they cannot keep it and I think the
reason is that they let it get too dry and do not divide it regularly. Left to itself it gets rather woody, too many crowns
develop from one root and when that root fails to get enough
moisture the plant is doomed. Another way to deal with it is to
top dress it with a good sandy compost so that the crowns make
their own new and thrusting roots and become separate plants.
I often top dress those in crevices and the others often get divided at least twice a year, if I have time and the weather is moist.
The newly divided plants, however, arouse the curiosity and
greed of the birds. I imagine they hope to find worms when
they remove the newly planted divisions, certainly it is quite
common to find half one's little plants lying gasping on top of the
soil, in spite of deep planting and a final firming with the flat of
one's foot.

The white counterpart of Dresden China, called The Pearl in
the South of England and Robert in Scotland, seems to have a
less robust constitution even than Dresden China. I have
introduced it into the garden half a dozen times and I do not
suppose there is now more than one rather half-hearted clump
left.

I have a little single daisy with narrow crimson petals and a
large yellow centre that came to me from Ireland but so far I
have not been able to find a name for it. It is very pretty and
blooms early and late—there are often flowers in the winter—

but it does not increase very fast with me and the divisions need careful watching. I think one really should take more trouble sometimes with plants. My usual way is to perform the dividing operation whenever I happen to notice that a plant is divisable and the weather is not dry. Sometimes I give the divisions a good start by adding peat and coarse sand to the soil, but I know I should do better if I potted up the little plants until they are really established. But that all takes time and there is never enough time to do all one wants in a garden.

There is a very good double pink daisy called Mavourneen, a little bigger than Dresden China and in not such a salmon-pink. It is altogether darker in colour. It came to me from Scotland, but I imagine it came from Ireland first. Bon Accord is another pink, bigger than the other two, with fleshy leaves and deep rose flowers. It is a thick and sturdy plant and with me it has settled down well between stones at the edge of the drive.

The crimson daisy Rob Roy is a typical cottage garden plant, gay, strong and flowering for a very long time. I divide it because I want to increase my stock, but I think it would get on quite well even if it were not touched for a year or two just as the big double daisies do. It has fairly big flowers and long stalks and is very much at home among herbaceous plants. I like to use it in my very mixed borders by planting it in wedge-shaped blocks against the stone paths that divide my flower beds, and by the end of the season the daisies have increased sufficiently to make a very solid mat, through which no weed can penetrate. Alice is the pink counterpart of Rob Roy, rather salmon-pink in colour and not a very good doer. I have lost the lady several times in very dry weather when there simply has not been time to look after everything. Mount Etna is another daisy about the same size as Rob Roy and Alice, perhaps a little bigger, but it can be used in the same way. The petals are a brilliant crimson and quilled.

The Hen and Chickens Daisy (*Bellis prolifera*) is a very old plant and how it has survived to this day I really do not know. It grows best in damp, rich soil, with some shade and it should be divided regularly and top dressed occasionally if it is to remain in the family.

The one I grow has red-tipped, white petals which make it

look pink. There are references in old books to a white one, but I have never seen it. To begin with it looks like an ordinary double daisy and the first time it flowers there is considerable anxiety until the little swellings appear at the back edge of the flower. These develop into little pink daisies, perfect miniature reproductions of 'Mamma', and they are attached to her by thin stalks which grow to about a quarter of an inch. When all the little daisies are fully out the effect is of a very shaggy, rather untidy, flower. It is sometimes called Jackanapes on Horseback in old books.

Bellis aucubaefolia, a sport from *B. perennis*, was often grown in old gardens, and there are references in old books to this daisy with deep red, pink and white flowers. I was given it by a friend who found a large patch of it growing in her cousin's lawn. The leaves are mottled, like those of the aucuba, and the general effect is of a golden leaved plant. Mine has single white daisies, like our native daisy, so really it is only the leaves that make it worth growing, and those seem to lose much of their gold in the winter, so it is wise to plant it where it cannot be mistaken for an ordinary daisy, although if one looks at it closely the leaves are never as densely dark as the wild daisy. I have mine planted in a large crevice in paving, and to make sure that I do not lose it I have a few in a frame. I notice that in the winter, when the leaves of those planted outside are hardly gold at all, the ones in the frame are a brighter gold than even their summer plumage.

There is one tiny little daisy that is not really a daisy at all, although its name bellium has the same derivation as bellis, for *bellus* means pretty. *Bellium minutum* is indeed very small, and it is not a conspicuous plant for one almost needs a magnifying glass to see properly its tiny little flowers which have white petals backed with red. The leaves are very small and narrow, but what it has not got in stature it makes up for in determination. Put it between stones in paving—the narrowest crack will do—and it will work its way along as far as it can go, sending up a veritable forest of tiny leaves.

The old double and quilled daisies would look like giants beside this midget. Accounts of old gardens often include references to quilled daisies and these are available today and can easily be grown from seed. One strain called Pomponette has double flowers in all shades of white, pink and red. The flowers themselves are rather small—for double daisies—with quilled petals. Another quilled daisy called Fire King has bigger flowers, and there is a lovely salmon-pink quilled double that can be grown from seed and gives a delightful old world cottage-look to any garden.

Some of the giant double daisies have loose shaggy heads and they can be made quite a feature of the garden. The flowers of the strain called Enorma are very large, but they are close-packed and firm.

Many gardeners grow double daisies as biennials and raise fresh stocks each year, but I prefer to do as the cottagers do and leave my big double daisies in the ground from year to year, to multiply and seed themselves about. I find their progeny in paving chinks and tucked under low walls, at the side of the path and sometimes in the walls themselves. I never see any point in moving them for mine is a cottage garden and double daisies are certainly part of it.

12. Summer Beauties

There are certain flowers that one always associates with the thatch and warm brick of an old cottage. Hollyhocks are one of them, in white or pink or red, and many shades in between, double or single. There used to be hollyhocks with variegated leaves but I do not believe they exist today. In pictures of old cottages there are always hollyhocks, silhouetted against the old walls or standing sentinel beside the cottage door. They seed themselves most generously and there are always plenty coming on. In bigger gardens hollyhocks are often attacked by rust and have to be dug up and burnt, but the ones that grow in cottage gardens are usually more healthy.

Sunflowers (*Helianthus annuus*), are also typical cottage flowers with their great round country faces, which always seem too big for any plant, and are quite out of proportion to the rest of the picture. Why sunflowers were so popular I have never known, unless they were grown for the seed. They are very easy, of course, and very accommodating in a tiny garden for they do their flowering way above the other garden inhabitants. You certainly get a lot for your money and there is something very rural about those great moon faces looking so haughtily over the high fence.

The May flowering peonies were other prized plants and really they have much to recommend them. Modern peonies have flowers in many delicate shades and they are ravishingly beautiful but they do not last nearly as long as the various forms of *P. officinalis*. There is a cottage in the next village where great clumps of double red peonies grow on each side of the door, and those patches of glorious colour are there for all to enjoy for nearly a month. Nothing could look better against the mellowed stone of the old cottage. The popular name of this peony, *P. officinalis rubra plena*, was Pianet. There are also

70

white ones and pink ones, all sweetly scented. The ones we grow today are all doubles, and I do not know what has happened to the singles—white, pink and crimson—which are mentioned in old books. There used, also, to be one so dark that it was almost black and was rightly called La Negresse. The double anemone-flowered peony was a rich crimson and had irregular petals. The old double white opens a flesh pink and becomes white as it ages and the double rose pales to a rich blush-pink.

Peonies are wonderful plants for labour-free gardens and although the greatest demand today is for Chinese peonies, the old European plants have come in for a little attention because of their stalwart habit and earlier flowering.

The old double Day-lily, *Hemerocallis fulva*, was another favourite. It needed no attention and came up year after year, producing its daily offering of flowers for many weeks. It is a soft orange and blends happily with other flowers.

The tall blue spikes of Jacob's Ladder (*Polemonium coeruleum*) rise gracefully from attractive ferny foliage. This is the polemonium that is associated with cottage gardens, usually in blue but very occasionally in white. It seeds itself enough to keep the strain going, but never enough to be a nuisance. My complaint against the ordinary Jacob's Ladder is that the flowers at the top of the spike have always finished before the bottom ones open, and the flowers themselves are rather small compared with *P. richardsonii*. I have a dwarf lavender-pink polemonium which I was given from a little garden in a neighbouring village which I think is a far better plant than *P. coeruleum*. The foliage is dark and evergreen and the loose sprays of open flowers are carried on 9 inch stems. It flowers on and off all the summer and spreads until the individual clumps become a dense carpet of green. There is a blue form but it is not so good in any way, although I would not be without it in the garden. The pale flesh pink *P. carneum* is very graceful and delicate in colour, and is very seldom seen. Some of the polemoniums flower once and once only. The little hybrid Blue Pearl is very pretty during its brief flowering and so is the exquisite little *P. pulcherrimum*, with its light blue flowers. The yellow *Polemonium flavum* is a biennial but it sows itself sufficiently for a small planting each summer. The flowers are rather a dull shade of yellow, and the plant is long and thin, compared with the others. As a plant I would not bother about it but as a member of the polemonium family I want it.

I remember a nurseryman offering me *Stokesia laevis* (syn. *cyanea*) more than twenty years ago with the remark that it is a very old plant. It is, and a very charming one with large lavender-blue flowers that bloom for weeks on end. I still have the plant I bought all those years ago. It has not increased much and I have never done anything about propagating it. But I like to have it in the garden and I regard it as a friend just as I do bits of furniture that have been in the family for a very long time.

I put the Woundwort (*Stachys* or *Betonica grandiflora superba*) in the same category. It is a good furnishing plant with its thick comfortable evergreen leaves and stiff spikes of rosy-purple. Its old name of The King in Splendour is a good one as it has a sumptuous regal look when at the height of its beauty.

Lychnis chalcedonica (Jerusalem Cross) is one of the few plants I find it difficult to place in the garden. The hard orange-red of its flower does not mix well with any other colour, and yet it never jars in the jostling crowd of a cottage garden. The cottagers like even better the double red lychnis, which doubles the dose, but I think this flower loses something in its double form, for the flowers are rather smaller and not so regular.

Though the bright magenta-pink of the sticky *Lychnis viscaria splendens plena* is even more intense it is a good mixer with the right plants. It makes quite a sensation against the grey-blue of *Nepeta* Souvenir d'Andre Chaudron or the slaty flowers of *Scutellaria canescens*. Even the fleeting spikes of *Veronica gentianoides* look impressive against the magnificence of this showy lychnis.

I find it difficult to find the right place for tradescantia in my own garden because it likes sun above and damp below—it is untidy for a border and not quite a wild plant—but it looks quite at home in little tightly packed gardens. The three petalled flowers are beautifully formed and they come in so many different colours, which are all lovely. It is well-named the Trinity Flower, or Moses in the Bulrushes, and its tangle of stems and leaves are no doubt responsible for its most common name of Spiderwort.

No cottage garden would be complete without columbines (aquilegias), the old fashioned Granny's Bonnets, with neat little heads in blue, soft pink and purple. Columbines do not like to be too dry, but beyond that they do not mind if they grow in shade or sun and they sow themselves almost too generously. But their foliage is so beautiful, even without their flowers, that one puts up with it. Hensoll Harebell is a good form of *A. alpina* breeding true from seed. It has flowers of soft blue with golden centres. It has adopted one bed in my garden, and I let it do what it likes there. A lot of people ask for it, so that I can keep myself from being swamped, and it is so lovely that I am grateful for its sea of blue.

Another old flower in soft blue called Blue Thistle that does well in a mixed garden is a member of the lettuce family *Mulgedium* or *Lactuca bourgaei*. It grows rather tall and has soft blue flowers above very handsome light green leaves. It seeds about the garden but not to a very irritating extent.

One could find almost any geranium in one of these old gardens, from the blue meadow geranium, *G. pratense*, to the violent *G. armenum* (*G. psilostemon*), in bright cerise with a black eye. *G. sanguineum*, having got a foothold, would be slowly encroaching on others and opening its magenta flowers in every month in the year, and there might be *G. renardii* with soft grey-green leaves and pale, pencilled flowers. But the most usual one would be *Geranium ibericum*, about two feet high and with the most intense blue flowers. It does not have a long season of blooming but when it is in flower it is really a magnificent sight. Afterwards it is not so good because it gets untidy and is messy for a long time, but grown in a jungle one does not notice. Another likely one is the woodland geranium, *G. phaeum*, sometimes called Little Niggers and also appropriately enough Mourning Widow because of its dark, almost black flowers, that flutter on slender stems. This is the Dusky Cranesbill of our hedgerows and though the flowers are small and dense in colour it flowers so freely that it is by no means dull, and the form with white flowers is just as attractive in a different way.

The first time I became conscious of *Stachys lanata* was just after I had started gardening. With a new and bare garden I was a constant visitor at the local nursery and one day the proprietor asked if I could help him. He had had an enquiry for *Stachys lanata*, so often called Lamb's Ears or Jesus Flannel, and thought that it might possibly be found in the garden of some cottage in my village. That shows how little was thought of our ubiquitous silver plant twenty years ago. And even now some gardeners are superior about it. Recently I read in a book that it was a plant beloved of children and despised by experts!

We have come a long way since then. The first silver plant one thinks of is *Stachys lanata*. It makes a lovely edging; it falls over the edge of a wall with grace, and can be used as a carpet or a border plant. Some people cut off the tall branching spikes with their embedded mauvy-pink flowers, but they are excellent when something emphatic is needed. I am always torn between garden and house. I love to see a bold group of this plant in the garden but I also like to have a few dried spikes in the house during the winter.

The lilies that grew in cottage gardens used to be the envy of all gardeners, I say 'used' because they are not so often seen now. In the old days rows of stately white lilies were a feature of every cottage garden. Owners of bigger gardens struggled to follow the treatment that made these lilies so happy in their modest homes and so dissatisfied with most ordinary gardens. *Lilium candidum* likes to be left undisturbed. It likes moisture and nourishment and resents being planted too deeply and must not be left out of the ground for long. We give ours all those things as well as love and attention, but seldom do they grow and flower with the ease and serenity as they used to in the little cottage gardens.

When we came to this house there were many Madonna Lilies growing happily against an old brick wall. The house had been two cottages and these were relics of the cottage gardens. I made a great fuss of them, because they were the perfect plants for the garden I visualised, but they did not think much of the way I scratched round their roots, removed the groundsel and bindweed which had become their boon companions, and laboured so hard to please them. I still have the lilies in different parts of the garden. There is magnificent foliage early in the year but seldom really good heads of flowers. This lily is, of course, very prone to disease, but even in its old healthy days it was never so good in the gardens of the big houses as it was in its happy, homely environment.

13. Old Favourites

Many of the plants most beloved by cottagers were very old and it is difficult now to find their correct names. To them they were just geums, or heucheras or penstemons and they did not know or bother about anything else. This simple naming would please the people who find the use of Latin names unnecessary. I have been asked several times if I will please use only the ordinary names in the next book I write, but unfortunately not all plants have everyday names, and there is no other way of identifying plants except to give their long and tiresome Latin names.

For years I have grown a very good geum that came from a cottage garden, but I have never been able to get its correct name. It is a big plant and as tough as one would expect, and the flowers on their two foot stalks, are a rich orange-yellow. It increases well and I must have given away hundreds of plants, luckily to people who generally do not worry about names. Another geum that one often sees in little gardens is *G. rivale* with its nodding heads in coppery-red. Avens is its country name and it probably has been brought in from the wilds. Some forms have larger, better coloured flowers, and I have one with bright cherry flowers. That plant too is going back to the little gardens from whence it came as it increases very fast. We do not have new cottages in the village any more, but plenty of modern bungalows and their owners are just as keen to fill their gardens as in the old cottage days.

The heucheras one saw were always red. They became woodier with the years and to see their gnarled and ancient limbs it seemed incredible that they could produce young leaves and sprays of crimson flowers each year. They may have been forms of *H. americana* or *H. sanguinea*, and though the flowers would be somewhat dingy beside the brilliant and diverse colours of our modern species they were a welcome sight

76

each spring. In the same way I remember dull red penstemons in the gardens of my youth, and pyrethrums with small flowers in shades of crimson which went on year after year without attention.

Most of the cottage plants flowered in their due season and then settled down for a year's rest, lupins and big red poppies, the Common Golden-Rod (*Solidago virgaurea*) and tawny heleniums. The irises that were grown were nearly always the ordinary purple 'flags', which flower more freely and earlier than many of our modern types. Monkshood was another favourite, probably our native plant, *Aconitum anglicum*, which flowers earlier than *A. napellus* and is a most handsome plant in its own right with fine spikes of helmeted flowers in deep blue, and dark green leaves.

There would always be a clump of phlox, not the large-flowered varieties we favour today, in dazzling shades of cerise and violet or ravishing pinks, but a rather hard purplish-crimson, and sometimes a washy mauve and white. It says a lot for the tenacity of these old plants that they existed without cultivation, getting woodier and more congested as the years went by. Bits might be broken off from the outside of the clump to give to friends or to make new gardens for the children as they got married, but I doubt if the plants were ever disturbed otherwise, certainly never lifted and divided as we regularly lift and divide our plants today.

Veronicas were popular plants, probably because they seed themselves so generously. I have several tall veronicas in my garden that are of the cottage garden type and I know I shall never lose them because of the odd plants I find in various parts of the garden. They may be forms of *V. spicata* and I bear with them and their descendants although their flowering season is so short. The dark blue dwarf veronica is a dazzling sight when in full bloom, with its eight inch flower spikes, but they start to drop in a very few days. I often wonder why the ordinary veronicas are so very prolific with their seedlings while the less common types seldom seed at all. The busy little carpeting veronica *V. filiformis*, is called Bird's Eye by country folk and is not despised by them. Admittedly it is an attractive little plant and it might get a better reception in our gardens today if it would be content to stay in one place and not attempt to carpet the whole garden.

Anchusa sempervirens has not the presence nor the big and plentiful flowers of present day anchusas but it was a welcome guest with its hairy leaves and twinkling flowers. Galega, or Goat's Rue, in pale mauve or white looks much like a Hedge Vetch but it makes a fine upstanding clump about three to four feet high and flowers for several weeks.

There is an old erigeron called *E. multiradiatus*, which is one of the toughest and most good tempered plants I know. In the rather cramped quarters of a cottage garden it would not have room to fling wide its long arms, with their branching stalks, and they would have to assume an upright position, which is the way in which they look best. Ever since I have had a garden I have grown this erigeron but it was a source of irritation to my husband until I learnt that it had to be trained early to hold up its arms. His criticisms were justified for left to itself it is an ungainly creature, but if supports are introduced as it starts to grow, it can be a worthy citizen of the border. It flowers for the whole summer and seeds itself in a quiet way. Colour variations occur in its progeny; my original plant has mauve flowers and the children are in shades of mauve, pinky-mauve and pink. The little pink *E. philadelphicus*, with its hanging heads and succession of flowers, seeds itself in odd places and fits into a country picture.

I expect all gardeners have been offered the blue *Centaurea montana* when they first started making their gardens. I was given it from a neglected rectory garden and although I have given it away, pulled it up and treated it brutally, I still have it. The kinder-hearted cottager would always find a place for it, however crowded his garden might be.

The perennial flax, *Linum perenne*, is one of our natives and it has found its way into many little gardens. It is a simple, graceful plant, with soft blue flowers on wiry stems and is most effective rising from stones at the edge of a path. Thrift, *Armeria maritima*, is another native plant that has great garden merit and makes a most satisfactory edging. Both *Pulsatilla vulgaris* (Syn. *Anemone pulsatilla*) and *A. nemerosa*, the Wood Anemone, grow wild in many parts of the country but they have great beauty and I am not surprised we often find them tucked away in humble gardens. *Pulsatilla vulgaris*, the Pasque flower, is most common in blue, and some interesting variations occur in the white *A. nemorosa*, for sometimes the flowers are double, or in another type have green ruffs behind the flowers. London Pride (*Saxifraga umbrosa*) grows happily in whatever dark corner it finds itself, flowering without complaint.

Bugles have admirable carpeting capacities and were welcomed to fill odd corners. The common lithospermum, *L. purpureo-caeruleum*, can become a nuisance if left to itself, for although the flowers are lovely in a deep shade of blue, they are quite overshadowed by the long leafy stems, which fling themselves out in all directions, settle down and root themselves into new plants, to start the game all over again. The usual colour of the Meadow Sage, *Salvia pratensis*, is deep blue but it sometimes produces flowers that are almost pink, and with these interesting variations it has real garden merit and gets invited into many gardens just as we find the Meadow Geranium, *G. pratense*, in varying shades, and the Dusky Cranesbill, *G. phaeum*, which has tiny flowers which are almost black.

The old perennial candytuft has less spectacular white flowers than the variety we grow today, but it still makes a snowy sheet in May, and its dark foliage, clambering over a wall, or falling across a path, is good all through the year. And so is the ferny foliage of *Filipendula hexapetala flore pleno*. The plants hug the ground and throw up two feet stalks topped first with pink buds which open to double cream flowers. It came to me from a cottage garden and I have since seen it making a most impressive corner plant in Lord Elphinstone's Scottish garden.

Thalictrum adiantifolium looks such an innocent plant with its delicate maidenhair leaves and slender sprays of greenish flowers. It makes a lovely background for other plants and the cottagers like to use it with their pansies for buttonholes and nosegays, but one should not be deceived by the fragile beauty above ground. Below it has the toughest, most determined yellow roots I know, and it will never give up, but spreads stealthily in all directions. The handsome striped grass that we know as Gardener's Garters (*Phalaris arundinacea picta*) spreads too but it does it in a more honest, straightforward way, and one deals with it firmly by planting it in an old bucket, without a bottom, and enjoys it without worry.

No cottage garden would be complete without a patch of Lily of the Valley in a shady corner, growing thicker every year, and filling the air with perfume. Lilies of the Valley hate disturbance and so do the big clumps of Christmas Roses, *Helleborus niger*, which flower so faithfully and generously. I think most of us try too hard with our Christmas Roses. The cottagers just leave them alone, and they flower far better and often earlier than they do for the rest of us. There are seldom other hellebores grown, although one might occasionally find our two native plants, *Helleborus viridis* and *H. foetidus*, both with lovely green flowers in the winter. So many good plants found their way into these packed gardens and one never knew what treasures one would find.

14. Double Flowers

A great many people feel that when a flower appears in a double form it often loses a great deal of its charm. I think that is so in many cases but nevertheless many plants that we would not grow in their single state are much appreciated when they become double.

Double flowers have always been popular with cottage gardeners. The double Sweet Rocket is a good example. I do not think many of us bother much about single Sweet Rockets, the countryman's Dame's Violets, although they are pleasant enough in a wild garden, with their delicate perfume and flowers of white or lavender. But the Double Sweet Rocket (*Hesperis matronalis flore pleno*) is quite another matter. We would all like to grow it but we usually have to go to a cottage gardener if we want to get hold of it.

I know small gardens where it flourishes. It appears year after year and can be divided like other herbaceous plants. I was once given a precious plant of the double white Sweet Rocket and I studied the instructions given in old gardening books about taking cuttings and though I followed them very closely I did not succeed with the material I had from my one small plant, which, of course, disappeared quietly after it had produced its flower.

According to the old books, the best way is to take off the flower stems when the flowers have finished and cut them into short lengths. If the bark is slit with a knife and separated from the stem around the base of the cutting it naturally curls up and appears to promote a tendency to produce roots. Mine merely had a tendency to do nothing at all, but if I can ever get hold of another plant I shall certainly try again.

There is something most attractive about these foot high spikes of double flowers that are delightfully scented. One is lucky to find a double white form nowadays, or a double mauve. About fifty years ago there were two others that were commonly grown, a dwarf white which came from Scotland and one called *purpurea plena*, which was dark purple in colour. Old writers refer to double red and double pink Sweet Rockets, but I have never met anyone who had a single 'Rocket' in these colours, let alone a double one.

The old double wallflowers are almost as difficult to keep, but I understand it is possible to propagate them in the same way as the Sweet Rockets. While Cheiranthus Harpur Crewe is not a difficult plant to increase, if one takes cuttings before they are old and woody, the old double yellow and double red are exceedingly difficult. Still someone must have been able to grow them for they have been cultivated in this country for at least three centuries.

Harpur Crewe is a most attractive plant and very well worth growing. It flowers early and it flowers late. It has a delicate scent and a good bushy habit, but it is not nearly such an old plant as the other two. It was discovered as a chance seedling in Scotland and is said to do best in dry walls, although I find it grows quite satisfactorily in an ordinary bed. It gets big and woody after a few years and is not able to stand up to the blustering winds of winter, because the root is really very small to carry such bulk, and when this happens it is the time to pull it out and start again with a small plant.

The old double yellow and double red are still in existence but only just. I sometimes feel like reversing the first two words when referring to the double red, Old Bloody Warrior. At his best he is a difficult and dessicated old gentleman, and needs a very special position in a hot dry bank. I expect he would enjoy a wall too, but I would not dare to experiment unless I had more than one plant, which is something that is not likely to happen.

The old double yellow is just as difficult and even more difficult to find, but the other three which I have read about, which sound delightful, have been lost to cultivation I fear. I have never heard of anyone growing the old double black, or the double pale yellow, or the most exciting one of all, a double greeny-yellow, which looked almost green. According to old garden writers, these veterans had very long spikes, from eighteen inches to two feet, and the flowers were densely double.

Luckily we still grow the double mauve Cardamine known by
country folk as Lady's Smock, Cuckoo Pint or Cuckoo Flower.
It is a favourite country flower and sees to it that it does not die
out. It increases by the leaves, which fall off and root themselves
to the ground, but unfortunately only a proportion of the children inherit their parent's double flowers. I find this rather a
nuisance as one has to allow all the seedlings to flower before
one can root out the mongrels. And there are a lot of seedlings,
round the parent plants and in other places. I imagine the single
plants manage to seed themselves in the normal way before I
have had a chance to bear down on them, and so there is a
tendency to get more and more single plants as time goes on.

The double Red Campion *Lychnis dioica fl. pl.*, is another very
good cottage plant. It prefers rather a shady position and then
makes itself into quite large mats which carpet the ground. They
are easily divided into smaller plants and the foliage is very neat.
It is so neat, in fact, that I once lifted and divided a clump and
sent it to a friend to whom I had promised the red daisy Rob
Roy. I admit I did it in a hurry and there is really no excuse for
such a mistake as the foliage is a different texture, but it turned
out well because my friend was delighted with her campion and
of course got the daisies afterwards as well.

The flowers of this campion are very gay and artless. They
grow on foot high stems and seem content to grow anywhere
and put up with any amount of neglect. I think they like to grow
close to other plants and do not mind if they grow right under-
neath a shrub, although the position I try to give them is light
shade. They are so good tempered that I fear one day I may
wake up and realise that they have been swamped by other
things. I try to divide all plants of this description regularly, but
sometimes I forget and luckily the campion bears no malice.

There is evidence that another old double flower has been
rescued from its obscurity in old gardens and is being cultivated
more widely. Its old names were White Bachelor's Buttons,
Fair Maids of France or Fair Maids of Kent and its botanical
name is *Ranunculus aconitifolius fl. pl.* It is by no means a
spectacular little plant, but it has great personality with its
small double white flowers and really lovely dark, cut leaves. It

prefers a damp situation and disappears completely after flowering, which I always find disconcerting in a garden as closely planted as mine. Left alone it comes up faithfully year after year, but it is easily overlooked by zealous diggers, which may be one reason why it is not seen more often in ordinary gardens. It needs a quiet place where it is not disturbed and that is why it has survived in the smaller gardens.

The sticky, double pink Lychnis (*L. viscaria fl. pl.*) is another old plant. The colour of its flowers is bright (some people might even call it crude) but it is a definite and clear colour and it is certainly an old plant of character. There are single forms in white, carmine and flesh pink but the flowers are much smaller and they appear quite insignificant beside the dashing brilliance of our double friend.

This is another plant that really needs dividing fairly regularly. I have grown it for years and did not think much about it until one day I discovered I did not have it in the garden any more. That gave me quite a shock and I knew I had only myself to blame. It gets rather woody after a bit and to keep it happy I think one should divide it every year so that it makes new roots. I am taking great trouble now to keep it, as it is one of the plants I should hate to be without.

The double buttercups I might lose any day, not by neglect but by super diligence on someone's part. I might even pull them out myself, although I know perfectly well where they grow. The bulbous type, *Ranunculus bulbosus fl. pl.* is quite distinct, with extra large and well marked leaves, but the creeping buttercup, *R. repens fl. pl.* is distressingly like the wild one in its habit of growth and the shape and general appearance of its foliage. Its flowers are smaller than those of the bulbous plant, little tight gold buttons which go well with the ordinary buttercup leaves. The double flowers of *R. bulbosus* are quite large and with a sheen that is almost metallic. There is a distinct greenish tinge in the centre and combined with the really beautiful foliage the plant is extremely handsome.

The little double-flowered form of the white saxifrage called *S. granulata* var. *plena* (so-called because the roots are composed of small nut like granules) was probably a freak plant of our native Meadow Saxifrage, which typically has single white flowers. I have seen it in many cottage gardens, where it is much beloved. I do not wonder for it is a perky little plant with its sprays of little white rosettes held proudly on six inch stems above rosettes of thick scalloped kidney shaped leaves. It disappears completely after flowering, which is disastrous in a well cultivated garden and I think the reason why we do not see it more often in bigger gardens is because of the disturbance to the root grains by the gardener's industrious trowel. And this is why it often pops up in quite unexpected places, quite unabashed. I read in an old book that *Saxifraga granulata* was the plant referred to in 'pretty maids all in a row', which were tended so zealously by 'Mary, Mary Quite Contrary'. I have not yet discovered which plant is meant by the reference to 'Silver Bells'. In Ireland they grow a little campanula which has a village name of Silver Bells and which I think is *Campanula planiflora*, but I have not been able to confirm that name.

The double flowered forms of *Geranium pratense* probably started their popularity by being grown in a cottage garden. The cottagers had no money to buy plants and they had to rely on gifts or 'finds'. Many of their treasures were discarded plants from the big house. When fashions in gardening changed, the old plants whatever their worth were thrown out to make room for new ideas. Luckily the cottagers were only too glad to have these unwanted flowers, otherwise many of them would have disappeared a long time ago. Other plants they grew were their own findings in the lanes and meadows. The meadow geranium is a beautiful plant and good enough for any garden, even in its normal shade of rich blue, and variations in colour were eagerly sought. The delicate silver blue which we now grow as *G. pratense* Silver Queen no doubt originated in this way, and the doubles also were probably discovered by some humble but zealous gardener. I do not know how many shades they had in the old days, I know of only two being grown today, a dark blue and a purplish blue, which is called purple in nurserymen's catalogues.

Double hollyhocks, of course, are still grown but I do not think the old named varieties exist anywhere today. They were killed by rust, and although one sees as many double hollyhocks as single ones they are rather nondescript and not nearly as effective as the single varieties. I have never seen the old double Martagon lily but I believe it is still grown. It was in existence as long ago as 1676 but appeared to be lost for some years until it was found growing well in an old garden in West Lothian. Nor do I know anyone who has ever seen the double hardy cyclamen.

The double Marsh Marigold was no doubt a casual discovery in the beginning and has been treasured ever since. There is something most alluring about Marsh Marigolds (*Caltha palustris*) sending up their thick juicy stems in damp meadows. The lacquered green leaves are akin to those of the lotus, and they belong so well to the fat round buds and large open flowers that might have been covered with gold leaf. They are spring personified, with hot sun and grass grown high, and blue skies above. All well loved flowers have many names. In Somerset I have heard Marsh Marigold called Gold Knobs and in Buckinghamshire they are Butter Clocks or Hobble-Gobble, while we all know them as Kingcups.

How the little dark crimson double Sweet William has survived all these years I do not know. Its full name is *Dianthus barbatus magnificus,* and it is known as King Willie. I am very fond of it and try hard to keep it but I have lost it more than once. It is a very old plant having been produced by a Scottish nurseryman in 1770. It was sometimes called Murray's Sweet William and at one time was immensely popular.

It is a low growing little plant, usually not more than six inches tall, and increases sideways in a series of heavily-leaved stems. They are rather liable to rot off at ground level when the plants get too big, so I think to keep one's stock going it is important to take cuttings every year as small plants seem to get on better. The foliage is bronze and when the plant is covered with flat heads of very dark crimson sweet scented double flowers it is a magnificent sight. They grow it better in Ireland than we do in England, great crimson carpets, which glow in the sunlight. I think it must like moisture as well as sun because in dry summers it may not attempt to flower at all and with me it can look most unhappy until it decides it simply cannot go on any longer.

We grow double violets today but our Parma violets are not

the double violets of olden days. There used to be a double form of the dark *Viola odorata*, which was particularly strongly scented. The double Duchesse de Parme is medium lavender and Marie Louise is slightly darker. It is not as deep in colour as the very old double violets which seem to have gone completely. I wonder which double white violet it is that Bacon refers to as flowering twice a year, about the middle of April and again about Bartholomewtide, and which he said had the sweetest scent of all. The only double white violet I know is Comte de Brazza. It is scented but it does not flower again in the autumn, at least not for me.

Somehow the blue double lobelia has survived, which means that someone has been taking cuttings year after year. It is pretty and old-world, and though it does not compare in beauty with the modern improved single lobelias it is a quaint little plant and should be in every old-world garden.

The double nasturtium has the same old-fashioned charm and is much more compact in its growth than the single-flowered trailer. It is rather prim and the deep pink-orange of its flowers is by no means strident.

For some reason double flowers seem to go with old gardens, they have a quaintness and a something that goes with sun-bonnets and print frocks. The double primroses which I have mentioned earlier, are a good example of this.

15. Uninvited Guests

No garden would be complete without some of the artless little annual flowers, certainly not a garden where chance seedlings are allowed to stay and flower in the spots they have chosen for themselves.

How the plants first arrive in the garden is a mystery, because the owners of these little gardens would not be likely to buy flower seeds, and how they find empty spaces in which to settle is even more mysterious. But there you will find them, the determined little plants that come up year after year without any encouragement from anybody.

I have quite a number of the same kind of plants in my own garden. I do not know where they came from in the first place, but I know I shall never be without them.

I am sure that I never bought seed of *Limnanthes douglasii* the American Meadow Foam but every year it produces a thick carpet of seedlings. The foliage alone is worthy of the space it takes, neat and fringed in a light, yellowish shade of green. The flowers are a delightful combination of silver and gold, and have that lacquered finish one notices in buttercups and Marsh Marigolds. The villagers call them Custard and Cream, and admire them very much, not only for their delicate beauty but also because they are attractive to bees.

Candytuft (*Iberis amara* and forms) is a typical cottage garden annual and an odd plant will often arrive by itself and will be left to make a nice bushy plant in white, pink or lavender. Not for these little gardens are the large heads of big flowers, which are the seedsman's pride today, e.g. Giant Snowflake with trusses about six inches long.

White alyssum comes up year after year when once there has been a plant in the garden. It is a perfect plant for a simple garden, it will squeeze itself in anywhere and makes a soft

88

edging beside the little path. Once there has been a lavender alyssum in the garden that too will come back year after year, like the swallows.

An usual annual was *Omphalodes linifolia*, Venus' Navel-wort, which was introduced from South-West Europe in 1748.

Cornflowers are always associated with small country gardens, not the kind we buy now with large heads in many different colours, but the small, blue flowers of the cornfield. Foxgloves, too, undoubtedly come from the hedges and woods, but how lovely they are with their straight spires of dull pink. Verbascums sow themselves too. The towering cream flowered *V. chaixii*, or the dwarf purple *V. phoeniceum* are often seen. The biennial Evening Primrose, *Oenothera biennis*, seeds itself to distraction, but the large pale-yellow flowers which open at night also add delicious perfume to the evening hours, and are not despised.

And there will always be marigolds. I have asked many country folk to tell me what flowers they remember in their earliest gardens, and they all say marigolds, for once you grow these plants you will always have them. I knew a child who thought there was something supernatural about her gardening efforts. Every year she was given a few, penny packets of seeds which she sowed with great care but whatever she sowed they all came up as marigolds! It never occurred to her that the seeds were in the ground before she started and nothing else would have a chance to grow. I do not think she really minded because there is something very satisfactory about these old friends with their rounded leaves, thick stems and cheerful flowers. The scent is clean and astringent and it reminds one of a healthy, happy countrywoman. I am referring, of course, to the ordinary single or double types, with deep yellow or orange flowers. The more exotic varieties are very old. French marigolds (*Tagetes patula*) were introduced in 1573 and African marigolds (*T. erecta*) about twenty years later, but they do not appear by themselves in the open and they need more care than the plain, ordinary ones.

Nasturtiums (tropaeolum) sow themselves as generously, and they give the same feeling of simplicity and abundance. Nasturtiums like rather a damp position and you find them appearing from behind a water-butt or cascading down a shady bank. The green seed pods of the nasturtium were a favourite pickle in the last century but I never hear of them being used now.

Forget-me-nots cannot be kept out of any garden and no one would want to banish them completely, although they are sometimes too generous with their offspring. I do not feel kindly towards them when I find seedlings coming up everywhere but when later they turn themselves into a haze of blue that fills every space and melts into the flowers around them I am grateful for their persistence. Love-in-the-Mist is generous too, but not so lavish. The lovely turquoise-blue flowers in their frame of green filigree are never in the way. The white-flowered form is almost lovelier but I do not think the casual seedlings often come white. They never have done so with me and one has to buy special seed to get white flowers. White Love-in-the-Mist was one of the plants that Gertrude Jekyll loved to see in the garden, and it is as beautiful as her other favourites.

The seed of balsam (impatiens) could come from anywhere, and what a really magnificent plant a full-grown balsam is, with its red stems, lovely foliage and exquisite flowers in white or pink. Country folk refer to the plant as Jumping Jack or Policeman's Helmet, and children never tire of bursting the quaint seed pods and seeing the seeds shoot out in all directions. In a big garden balsam can become a real menace, but in the small and crowded space of a cottage garden there is not room for many of these buxom plants to get all the room they need.

Canterbury Bells must seed themselves wildly otherwise how would they appear in these little gardens whose owners certainly never went to the trouble of buying seed or small plants. Cup and Saucer Canterbury Bells in white or pink or blue have an old world charm that makes them perfect plants for country gardens.

Honesty will certainly be there, for who can keep honesty out of a garden? I do not think many of us want to, although honesty can become too much of a good thing and needs a ruthless hand. I have seen some of the most beautiful coloured forms of honesty in simple gardens, rich, deep purple which is a great addition to any colour scheme. And the silvery moons are allowed to stay when their thin coverings have gone (and all the

seeds with them) to add their fluttering ghostly beauty all
through the autumn and winter.

Not all the little strangers that appear are annuals. I defy
anyone to control the cheerful and indefatigable Welsh Poppy
(*Meconopsis cambrica*), with its succession of bright flowers in
yellow and orange. It is quite irresponsible and yet it has great
grace and beauty, and its only fault is that there are too many
members of its family wanting to settle down in one's garden.
I do not know how long an individual plant would go on. I never
allow them to get big and benevolent. The long tap-roots take
firm hold and the only easy way of dislodging them is to tackle
them when young. I am now trying to establish the double
Welsh Poppy because it at least will not try to populate the
entire garden with its progeny, but I do not expect ever to
eliminate all the single-flowered plants.

That old favourite, Rose Campion, that used to be called
agrostemma and is now known as *Lychnis coronaria*, is another
standby of village life, and is popular in bigger gardens too. It
seeds itself here and there and the neat silver rosettes make
excellent ground cover. I always like the stiff geometric pattern
of its downy stems, which go on building up through the summer
like a meccano. Perhaps the purple-crimson flowers may be
considered rather hard by some people but their harshness is
softened by the silver background. There is a really lovely white
flowered form with a little pink eye in the middle of the flowers,
and a dwarf, rather bright pink, suitably called Cottage Maid.
Unfortunately, these two less usual members of the family do
not sow themselves very freely and they are not such regular
cottage garden inmates.

Some members of the pansy-viola family sow themselves in
odd places that they think want a little improving. The flowers
on these casual interlopers are never very large and are usually
in shades of blue or purple, but are very attractive as they work
their way round the stems of roses or tall perennials. The flowers
of Mr Bowles' black viola are very small and they are usually
dark blue and not black. But it seeds itself generously so once
you have it—it is yours for ever. The little green viola, Irish
Molly, with her dirty brownish face, does not seed itself, and one
has to take cuttings to keep it.

There is a great demand for the old-fashioned Lady's Mantle at the moment. Discriminating gardeners are discovering what the cottagers have known for years. *Alchemilla mollis* is a lovely plant with its beautifully shaped leaves and feathery little green flowers. The soft grey-green leaves are folded like a fan, and they open like a fan. The tiny green flowers are like miniature stars. It is a persistent seeder but it always seems to find places where it looks best—at the bottom of a wall or in a bare corner where there is hardly room for its roots. I never mind how many seedlings I find in the garden, for they are all welcome.

16. On the Walls

It is inevitable that every inch of a cottage wall is covered with some kind of flowering plant, and not only the walls of the cottage but porches and arches. Porches are very important in these small homes, for with the front door opening right into the living room, winter winds can make the place very draughty. The porch can be made of wood or iron with trellis over it on which to train the plants. Sometimes the porch will be a living one, built up from Winter Jasmine, Box or *Lonicera nitida*, religiously clipped until it is thick and symmetrical. Trellised arches are very much loved, either at the side of the cottage or over the gate. They too will be covered with climbing plants, so that one enters under a floral arch into a veritable bower of colour and perfume.

Probably the most favoured of all climbing plants is the winter-flowering jasmine, *Jasminum nudiflorum*. When it is used to make the porch over the cottage door it has to be clipped constantly and one does not get so many flowers as when it is allowed to grow without restraint, but there are flowers on and off all through the winter. A cottage on the other side of the road from me has such a porch. It is four and a half feet deep and represents years of careful training. It is always a cheerful sight in the winter, and for the rest of the year the bright green stems and shiny leaves are a constant pleasure.

One reason why one sees this jasmine so often is, of course, on account of the ease with which it propagates itself. It is like the blackberry and spends its time trying to get the ends of its long trailing stems into the earth, where they quickly make a nice little bunch of new roots. And that is not the end of its efforts for every stem that finds itself lying along the ground proceeds to root itself at every joint. No wonder we see winter jasmine on so many walls, but never too many for me, for how cheering are its little sprigs of yellow flowers with buds suffused with orange, that bloom on the bare stems in mid-winter. It will grow in any position but I think produces more flowers on a sheltered wall in good soil.

The summer-flowering jasmine (*Jasminum officinale*) is almost as popular. In my childhood every cottage had a little house down the garden and this was romantically smothered with the plant. I could not resist copying the idea when we bought our house. The little hamstone building made a useful home for tools and bass, bags of fertiliser and bamboos, but after some years the dreadful old door fell off its hinges and then I did what I should have done years before, turned it into a summer house. We left the walls on the North and East, and removed all but the lower part of those on the South and West. With a stone seat round two sides and its nice stone floor there is a pleasant little retreat for my guests.

The jasmine is planted on the North wall, there is a *Clematis jackmanii* on the East, and the old rose Gloire de Dijon goes clambering up over the roof.

I have many jasmines more refined than the old *J. officinale*, but none give me such pleasure as my old friend. I rejoice when the white buds start to open, and I am never without them in the house. There is no problem to decide what to use for the little bedside nosegays for my guests during the several months that the jasmine is in bloom. Its flowers may not be so big or so delightfully flushed with pink as the improved types but there are many more of them and the scent is far stronger. I do not wonder that many of the old cottages were smothered with this plant, growing right up into the thatch and framing the little bedroom windows.

If there is room for it to make a loose tangle, it is only necessary to secure the main stems to the wall. This is not as untidy as it sounds because it can be cut back really hard in early spring without spoiling its flowering. It likes to layer itself whenever it can by attaching the lower branches to the ground with new roots.

Honeysuckle is a close second to the jasmines and makes a beautifully scented covering for an arch or porch. Inevitably, forms of our native Honeysuckle or Woodbine, *Lonicera periclymenum*, are most usually seen and they do remarkably well because so many of the little cottages can offer a moist, shady position, which this plant loves.

The evergreen honeysuckle, *L. japonica*, particularly the golden variegated var. *aureo-reticulata*, is seldom seen today, except in cottage gardens. Its curiously 'netted' leaves strike an old world note and it is a pity that this plant, which used to be so generally grown, has rather taken a back seat in recent years. Not long ago I noticed it on a cottage near Stroud. The day was grey and cold but the honeysuckle struck a most cheerful note and I felt I was greeting a long lost friend.

The Everlasting Pea, *Lathyrus latifolius*, has a Victorian atmosphere about it and is one of the climbers most frequently found in little old gardens. It may be difficult to establish in the first place but once it has taken hold nothing will dislodge it. But who wants to? The rather crude magenta-ish-pink of the flowers may be a little strong for some people but it looks right in a cottage garden, and there is, of course, also a white form. The tangle of green merges pleasantly with the other plants growing up the walls, it flowers on and off for weeks on end and is quite capable of looking after itself.

Sometimes one sees a passion flower entwining itself among the other plants. These plants are not as difficult as many people think and produce suckers from which new plants are started, which is probably the way they get into cottage gardens. In summer there will be Canary Creeper, *Tropaeoleum peregrinum*, smothering everything in sight, and in early spring its seedlings may appear in many places to be trained against any blank walls. Sometimes one even sees that strange creature, *Aristolochia macrophylla* (syn. *A. sipho*), the Dutchman's pipe, with its strange green flowers.

Berberis aquifolium is a very good natured shrub which likes the companionship of an old wall. First it may be content to grow against it, but very soon it gets into it and comes out in many different places. We found one growing in and out of the East wall which surrounds our little front garden against the road. It tries to get into the bed as well, but I discourage it from burrowing among my hydrangeas and hellebores. In the wall it is a pleasant sight with glistening green leaves and bright yellow flowers, but I know it is slowly undermining the old wall.

I wonder why people in bigger houses do not occasionally grow hops (*Humulus lupulus*). I am meaning to grow a hop on one of my walls, the leaves and tendrils are nearly as beautiful as those of the vine and it takes admirable care of itself, finding its own means of support and producing most fascinating 'cones' in early autumn. Of course it is a fast worker and it would be disastrous to put it next door to a shy little plant. I think it was Darwin who timed the working of the hop and discovered that a twining stem made a complete revolution in two hours and eight minutes. At that rate one ought to be able to see it moving!

Vines are even more beautiful and I expect many that frame the windows and doors of the old cottages came from prunings from the greenhouses of the big houses. Except on a South wall in a sheltered district there are not likely to be many grapes, but most of us, I think, grow vines for the beauty of their grey-green leaves and the fascinating habit of stalk and tendril.

A fig takes up quite a lot of room but that would not stop one being planted on those overcrowded little walls. I have never heard of a fig tree in a cottage garden bearing fruit but it is much esteemed for the fluttering shade of its attractive leaves. The leaves themselves would always be carefully arranged on the plates that were to hold such fruit as raspberries and straw-berries.

Virginia creeper and wisteria are rather vigorous climbers for small buildings but that would not keep them out of the cottage gardens. A wisteria is capable of great things and it is nothing for it to travel all the way round a house and come back to the spot where it started. I am sure it is not the best thing for the house, although in some cases it may hold the old walls to-gether. I have several wisterias growing on different walls and so long as they do not get involved with roofs and gutters I do not think they do any harm. I am grateful for the help of one to hide the ugliness of a ventilating pipe. The plant has coiled itself round and round the pipe so that in summer it is completely ruffled with green and no longer an eyesore.

Sometimes one sees an unexpected plant on a humble home. *Euonymus radicans variegatus* makes a delightful symphony in pale green and cream. Years ago I was given cuttings from one growing on the walls of the garden of Brympton d'Evercy near Yeovil, one of the most beautiful houses I have ever seen. It also grows on the wall of a cottage in this village. I never noticed fruits on the one at Brympton d'Evercy, and certainly I have never had any on mine, but I have seen delicate shrimp-pink berries on that plant on the cottage wall.

Penstemon cordifolius from southern California is a connoisseur's plant. It is seldom seen and I believe is not too hardy; at any rate, we are recommended to plant it by a South wall. It is trained over the porch of a very old cottage in a village near here. The cottage faces North and yet the penstemon reaches six feet or more and is covered with bright red, tubular flowers all through the summer.

The red 'Japonica' (*Chaenomeles*) is another favourite. It is often grown as a bush but I think its most popular role is as a climber. The blooms appear so early in the year that the shrub can be trained to the lower part of a wall and it will not matter much if it gets completely hidden by greenery when the other plants in the garden recommence growth.

You will always find roses against old cottage walls. Some of the roses are so old that it is impossible to give them a name. I have such a rose in my own garden. It was growing against the garden wall when we bought the house and I cannot discover any other name except Gold and Silver, which is the village name for it. The small flowers come in bunches and are literally gold and silver. They are very sweetly scented but individually they do not last long. It is not a rose to cut but its perfume and the sparkle of its little flowers are enjoyable for several weeks each year.

Great Maiden's Blush grows against several of the cottages in this village. In one it has made a high bank of grey-green foliage against which the delicate pink flowers show up ravishingly. The same rose is growing in my own front garden. It must have been there for at least a hundred years and has survived many upheavals. The front garden, where I found it, was completely remade by us twenty years ago but the rose paid no heed and carried on flowering against the wall. There is also an old deep pink cabbage rose on the same wall.

The China, or monthly rose is another old favourite; usually it is one of the pink forms that is grown, and there are blooms in every month of the year. One was growing beside the garden door when we bought this house and I have heard from old people in the village that it had been there for at least a hundred years. I have since introduced the old green rose, which is an old kind but new to my garden. Not everyone shares my enthusiasm for its crumpled green and crimson, but if you forget that it is a rose and think of it as an unusual and interesting flower, that might well have come out of an old 'flower piece', it is well worthy of a place in the garden.

Moss roses, luckily, are coming back into favour. They have an old world look about them and are typical of these gardens. Occasionally one might find a double white damask rose, or the interesting striped York and Lancaster, and there might even be Marechal Niel on a sheltered wall, with his pale greeny-yellow flowers. One seldom sees this rose even in a greenhouse, but I remember it at my childhood home growing up an outside wall and flowering quite well. This was in a garden near London so perhaps it is not as tender as people think.

The favourite rambler, inevitably, is that irrepressible maiden Dorothy Perkins, with her shrill pink flowers and distressing habit of becoming mildewed at the slightest provocation. But she is gay and tireless and I can understand that her great cascade of colour was welcome. When we bought our house the so-called garden was so full of Dorothy Perkins that we were able to supply enough to a friend to make a hedge.

The clematis one sees most often is the dark blue jackmanii, which seems susceptible to mildew too. Clematis do not as a rule do very well on cottage walls as they are treated too kindly. Clematis of the jackmanii type have to be cut down in February when they have often made quite a lot of growth. It always hurts me to cut off the stems, but to the cottager it would be sacrilege.

I never know whether the ivy one sees on cottage walls is there by accident or design, but knowing the ways of ivy I am not in much doubt. I do not think ivy ever has such a good time as in a cottage garden, where it is allowed to wander as it will. It does a magnificent job on old tree stumps or bits of ruined wall that may be in the garden. I have heard that it only starts to flower when it stops climbing, and that is why one sees the great displays of attractive green flowers on the tops of old walls. The black berries that come later are just as lovely, but I like the five-lobed leaves of the non-flowering part of the plant better than the rather clumsy ones that grow on the flowering branches. But all ivy is beautiful, and I can understand how it is allowed to stay when it pokes its nose into a cottage garden.

17. Trees and Shrubs

In the tiny packed space of a cottage garden there is not much room for trees and shrubs, but there will usually be two or three. And very often one will be an elder (*Sambucus nigra*).

The elder tree has many uses and though most of us spend our gardening lives removing seedling elders from the garden, it is definitely a tree of character, which looks at home against old buildings.

It is easy to understand how it gets into all these village gardens. I think some birds must live entirely on the berries of elder and bramble judging by the number of seedlings one finds. I do not allow a single specimen of the ordinary elder to remain in the garden; if one wants the flowers or berries of elder one does not need to look very far in a country district.

The elder's usefulness begins when the blooms open; bunches of flowers tied in muslin and boiled with gooseberries give a delicious tang to gooseberry jam. When the fruit is soft the elder flowers are taken out and the sugar is put in. The dried flowers, mixed with dried peppermint, make an old country remedy for any kind of inflammation. While mint tea was used for colds and sore throats, mint and elderflower infusion was made to reduce inflammation, whether in the head, feet, body or arms. Elderberries, of course, make excellent wine and give a pleasant winy tang to apple jam. The wood burns well and as one needs to keep an elder within bounds there is always some wood for burning.

Try hard as I do to keep the common elder out of the garden, I am often nearly thwarted. Nature cunningly plants the seeds where the seedlings can develop without being observed, just as insects lay their eggs near a source of food supply. I find little elders growing right out of the middle of a big fuchsia or among the lower branches of a berberis, and they are sometimes quite big by the time I discover them.

The double flowered elder, of course, does not seed and the flowers are much more beautiful than the wild variety. I grow two variegated forms which I think are highly decorative. The silver variegated one has an unearthly quality which makes it a good choice for a dark corner, and the other, which is more speckled than variegated, is lighter still and is as good as a clump of white flowers if one needs something to tone down brilliant yellow or orange. I have not fallen for the golden variety yet, as I feel it may have many of the bad characteristics of the ordinary wildling, although many plants and trees with golden foliage are far less rampageous. There are many ways of getting golden leaves into the garden and I do not think I need go to the elder to get my splashes of gold.

Although the Snowberry (*Symphoricarpos*) grows in many a hedgerow it is a well-loved cottage plant, and sometimes there are whole hedges of it in tiny gardens. Its country name is Snow in Harvest, but the glistening white fruits swing from the slender, whippy stems long after the corn is threshed, sometimes till December. The berries are most attractive if cut for the house and I used to leave my self-sown Snowberries for this reason, but I admit I have far less patience than my cottage friends and I got tired of its suckering ways. But this is a case where you can have your cake and eat it because there is now a good cultivated form called White Hedge, which has particularly fine white fruits and it does not run. The white berries hang in big clusters like the large artificial pearls our grandmothers wore in bunches on their bosoms. The soft pink fruits on another Snowberry called Mother o'Pearl are borne in twos and threes and the bush has a nice sideways habit which makes it good for growing under trees.

Many years ago I was given a golden Snowberry from a little garden in the village. The leaves are a rather soft colour and are speckled with black or green. It makes a nice golden mound among the flowers of summer but when the leaves drop I have always felt it had no winter interest and I waited anxiously till I could cut it back in early spring. But now it has started to cover itself in autumn with tiny brilliant crimson berries. They are of different sizes and thickly encrust the stems so that the bush looks as though it had been decked with tiny crimson beads. This harvest first came after a very hot summer and also after I had trimmed the bushes more drastically than usual in the spring. So I am now left wondering what was the cause of this largesse. I shall repeat the heavy trimming dose but I would not arrange another hot dry summer even if I could. It may be, of course, only a matter of age. My bushes are now about twenty years old, but I cannot imagine a modest little bush like the Snowberry taking so long to make up its mind.

Apart from fruit trees—and there is almost certain to be an old gnarled apple tree, perhaps a pear or a plum, and some gooseberry and currant bushes—the most usual flowering trees to be found in these little gardens are May Trees or laburnums. Both have a simple artlessness which goes with old flowers, and probably started as chance seedlings, and of course were left to grow where they happened to find themselves.

I have noticed that most of the trees and shrubs one finds in such gardens are those that seed themselves freely. *Daphne mezereum* is a very industrious seeder but no one minds how many little bushes appear. The smother of orchid-pink or white flowers on the bare twigs in December and January is always a welcome sight and the sweet scent that comes wafting on the wintry air. I imagine the birds distribute the seeds as the little newcomers turn up a long way from the parent bush. Certainly the birds are very partial to the seed of *Daphne mezereum* and know just when it is best to eat. One day the bush will be covered with big red berries and the next morning every one will have disappeared. The yellow berries of the white daphne cannot be so tasty as they do not disappear in the same way— the little seedlings I find are always quite close to Mother and not scattered all over the garden.

Another daphne that seeds itself generously is *D. laureola*, our native green-flowered shrubby species. The more choosy gardeners would not give house room to this humble plant but I would not be without it. I like its shining evergreen foliage which is so neat and so very dark, and the delicate green blooms that flower close to the stem in February. The flowers are small but they have a delicious perfume and are well worth looking at closely. This shrub grows wild in parts of Dorset, and I have seen it used most attractively in flower arrangements with all the leaves removed. Then one can see how beautiful are the waxy-green flowers, and one would never recognise it for the same plant. When it does its seeding I do not know. I have never noticed seed on my plants, probably because I have never looked for it. It is such an unobtrusive plant that it melts into the landscape when it is not in bloom. I get a few seedlings but many people get more. There is one little cottage garden which is able to supply a big nursery with all the small plants needed for grafting the more aristocratic daphnes.

Most of the trees and shrubs one finds in the little gardens are either grown from cuttings or put themselves there. Myrtle is far from hardy and many of us have to plant it in a very sheltered spot or see it browned and desiccated every winter. A crowded garden offers more shelter and up against the house this delicate shrub may easily get on quite well. It was an accepted custom to plant sprigs from a wedding bouquet, myrtle, orange blossom and rosemary. Many of the myrtle bushes came into being this way. I have one myself that came to me secondhand in a cutting from a wedding bouquet bush. It flowers well in a good year and after a hot summer is covered with the most pleasing large black berries, growing upright on the branches, with a beautiful blue bloom to make a harmonious picture. I was looking at an old print in a cottage recently. It was drawn in the form of a sampler, with words and pictures. The title was 'The Language of Flowers' and though some of the pictures were difficult to determine I was able to recognise myrtle and was not surprised that its message was 'Love'.

Euonymus used to be greatly favoured as a bush, particularly the golden or silver variegated forms. Then we came to despise it and it was relegated to the same category as the despised privet. I remember that when we bought our house the garden at the back was still the same as it had been when the house was divided into two cottages. The 'pièce de resistance' in one little garden, in fact the only plant that was growing in it, was a large rounded bush of *Euonymus japonicus aureus*. My husband and I assumed, without even discussing it, that the first thing to do was to remove the harmless *euonymus*. I am certain I should have acted differently today. After twenty years of trying to create a garden with enough attractive evergreen shrubs to give it a warm, clothed look in winter I should not have despised that plant.

We have, alas, lost the simplicity and single-mindedness of the cottage gardeners who did one thing at a time and did it well. I often pass a cottage in the front garden of which are two of the best specimens of golden variegated holly I have ever seen. I believe both were grown from cuttings, and they have been carefully tended and groomed ever since. One is the rare and very prickly Hedgehog Holly, *Ilex aquifolium ferox aurea*, and the other, I think, *ovata aurea*. I go out of my way to admire these two bushes and wish I had the patience and perseverance to produce similar ones. Anyone who has tried knows that the Hedgehog Holly is very difficult to increase from cuttings, and once rooted plants take a very long time to become a reasonable size.

A well spurred bush of red 'japonica' (no self-respecting cottager would ever call it anything else and chaenomeles as a name would mean nothing) is a very satisfactory shrub. There is attractive foliage for most of the year, and while the rest of the garden is still asleep its bare boughs will be bright with blood-red, rounded blossoms.

Another shrub that is often found is the double *Kerria japonica fl. pl.*, called Jew's Mallow in the villages. It has tight little rosettes of flowers of rather a hard orange colour. For myself, I prefer the single-flowered kerria, with paler, open flowers and a graceful spreading habit. I also grow one with variegated leaves, which is perhaps more beautiful. But both these shrubs take up rather a lot of room, and the stiff upright stems of the double kerria are undoubtedly the best choice for a crowded little garden where every inch of space must be used.

In our pursuit for new and interesting types among the viburnums we are likely to overlook two very good, if old, varieties. Laurustinus, *V. tinus*, is a wonderful shrub for any garden, with its handsome dark foliage and smothering of pink-tinged white flowers so early in the year. The Guelder Rose, *Viburnum opulus*, is too good a tree to leave out of any but the smallest gardens, but the gardens of the cottages would find room for it somehow. Before the flowers are fully out they are delightful pale green balls, much prized by flower arrangers, and later when the tree is laden with its snowballs in glistening white it is a sight indeed. Its Somerset name is May Ball Tree. Laburnums seem to belong to cottage gardens too—often they arrive from seeds dropped by birds—and they are quite happy in shade.

There is one fuchsia that is hardy and is often found in cottage gardens. *F. magellanica* does not mind where it grows and often puts itself in an old wall. I found three in our garden, one was a big bush growing lustily in the small garden at the back, another was under a north wall in the front and the third sprang from a south-east corner in the front of the house, seemingly growing in a piece of stone. I have since tried to induce the variegated form of this plant to grow from a wall, but it is an independent creature and will not be coerced.

18. In the Cottage Window

When we first came to live in Somerset, just before the last war, every cottage window in the village was crammed with pot plants. In my ignorance I felt that this was very wrong, and did not hesitate to say so. The rooms were very dark, with low ceilings, often made darker by heavy beams, and the windows were always small. They were shrouded by curtains and then there were all the plants, packed close together and pushed as close to the window as possible to get all the light they could.

I had come from a London flat, and although I took it as a matter of course that now we had a house in the country I should work in the garden, I had no idea then of the fanatic I was to become. So it seemed criminal to me that all those misguided villagers should deprive themselves of light for a few potted plants!

Now, of course, I should have every sympathy with the plants, and would deprive myself of food, as well as light, if it was necessary for their well-being. I did not then realise how much those growing plants meant to their owners. Their gardens were small and they had to give more space to vegetables than flowers and the plants in the windows gave interest and companionship as they worked at their gloving.

There are very few cottages of the old type left in the village, and those that remain have been modernised and brought into line with the bungalows, villas and Council houses that are the people's choice today.

Some of the old plants are still grown; I see an occasional plant of the old type here and there but with improved conditions there is money to buy such things as cyclamen, coleus and primulas, and these have ousted the old favourites.

The zygocactus is one of the plants that is still grown. It is sometimes called the Christmas or Epiphany cactus because it flowers at that time of year. It is really a very attractive plant with its flat succulent stems, which keep adding sections to their length until at Christmas time each stem has dangling from its tip bright magenta-pink flowers, not unlike fuchsias. I was sympathising with the owner of one of these plants which had produced flowers on one stem only. She assured me that there had been beautiful flowers on the end of each stem but a naughty little robin had flown in through the window one sunny day and helped himself to nearly all the flowers. I am sure that this would never have happened in the old days because the windows were seldom, if ever, opened!

These zygocacti are the easiest plants in the world to increase. Every little bit of the flat fleshy stems will root, and it is surprising that not more of them are grown.

There used to be another type of cactus that was popular but not nearly so pretty. The Rat's Tail Cactus has long hairy stems that droop disconsolately over the edges of the pot. As they get longer and longer the pot has to be raised to give the gruesome tails enough room.

At first glance one would think that The Candle Plant (*Kleinia articulatus*) is a cactus, with its swollen stems, which look like green sausages standing on top of each other and sprouting curiously shaped leaves, but it is in fact related to groundsel! I believe it was first introduced into England in 1775 so it has been gracing our cottage windows for many a long year.

Bridal Wreath or Maiden's Wreath (*Francoa ramosa*) is not hardy everywhere and I expect that is why it was a favourite plant for the cottage window. In Somerset we grow it out of doors. I risk mine in a low wall, where it has to take its chance. Some people grow it in ornamental pots, which stand on a terrace or at the corners of a pool during the summer, and are taken into a sheltered place in the winter.

Out of doors the tall spikes of white or pink flowers are allowed to grow freely but in the cottage window they are trained on wire to make a hoop. This was done, I imagine, as otherwise the plants would be too tall for such a small space, and it, no doubt, was the origin of their country name. I have never heard of francoa being used for a bride's headdress although the neat little flowers and stiff stems would be very suitable for the purpose.

One of the plants I best remember in nearly every cottage window was Mind Your Own Business (*Helxine soleirolii*), bubbling out of its pot and pouring down the sides. I still see pots of helxine in greenhouses and sometimes on a window-sill, and I have never decided whether it is cherished in a pot because it is not quite hardy everywhere (although it is far too hardy in some gardens!) or that it is safer to confine it to a pot rather than let it loose in the garden. But whatever the reason it is definitely attractive grown in this way, and has the great quality of never having off moments.

It is a pity that it has no conscience out of doors because it is really the most perfect carpeting plant there is. It does the job most thoroughly, creeping steadily in every direction and smothering everything as it goes. It is a wonderful shade of fresh, bright green and its tiny leaves are exquisite. Its flowers are even smaller, I understand. I am ashamed that I have never taken the trouble to go down on my hands and knees with a magnifying glass to study them.

One hears it called by many names, Irish Moss, Irishmen's Wig or Paddy's Wig are some of them, but I do not know what connexion it has with Ireland. It is a native of Corsica and is sometimes referred to as Corsican Carpet or Corsican Curse; Japanese Moss is another name, and Creeping Nettle yet another. In America it goes by the name of Baby's Tears, but I think it might more correctly be called Gardener's Tears, so persistently does it plague us.

I am hoping that the golden helxine and the variegated helxine will show a little more moderation than the green form. In spite of a twenty year losing battle to keep the green helxine where I want it and not where it wants to be, I could not resist these two more unusual forms. So far the golden form is feeling its way in rather a suspicious manner, and I may have to remove it to a less valuable site. The variegated form is more timid, but then it is very young and does not know its way round yet.

The cottagers loved their pelargoniums and the brighter the flowers the better. They collected the ones with scented leaves as well, and the varied perfumes of rose or lemon, almond, peppermint or nutmeg filled their little rooms. They loved begonias too, begonias with great glowing flowers, and the lordly *B. rex* with its dark, richly fashioned leaves.

Saxifraga sarmentosa was another old favourite. This plant has attractive round leaves. It is a prolific breeder and earns its name of Mother of Thousands. Other names for it are Roving Sailor, Aaron's beard and Strawberry Geranium. Out-of-doors it spreads quietly in all directions, but in its pot in the window its young are not so comfortably catered for. It produces tiny plantlets on the ends of long, thread-like stems, and the poor little things dangle pathetically over the sides of the pot waiting for someone to adopt them. This saxifrage was introduced to this country from China and Japan in 1815, and in the days when there was often a conservatory leading out of the dining room or drawing room, it was a favourite plant for the front of the staging.

Tolmeia menziesii, sometime known as the Elephant plant, Pig-a-Back plant, Thousand Mothers and Youth-on-Age, has another way of dealing with its offspring. In addition to producing seed and being quite agreeable to division, it also creates little plants in each leaf. Out of doors—and I think this plant is quite hardy—the weight of the 'growing child' will bend the stem down to the earth and the little plant is satisfactorily launched in the world. In a pot it cannot do this and its tendency is to go up and up. Whatever it does, this is a most interesting plant to watch, and I suspect proved a distraction to the glove-makers.

The handsome red flowers of the Scarborough Lily (*Vallota speciosa*) were often seen. In spite of its name it is a south African plant and life in a cottage window suited it well. It enjoys sunshine and warmth and should not be completely dried off. It likes to live rather high up in its pot and loathes disturbance. In fact, vallota does best when it is pot-bound. There are no draughts in a cottage window, and each plant was given every attention. The Scarborough Lily liked an occasional application of soot or manure water, and of course it got it. Offsets are produced by the Mother bulb on the surface and can be rescued and potted.

The kindest thing that could be done for aspidistras and Maidenhair Ferns was to put them outside when there was a gentle warm rain, as they are like the birds and enjoy a bath. When I was a girl these plants and other ferns were very popular and I can well remember the ritual of carrying out the many pots, that stood on a stand in a bay window, the moment gentle warm rain was observed. In dry weather the leaves of aspidistras were tenderly sponged with warm water, and I have no doubt the cottagers were just as solicitous. We are inclined to despise the aspidistra and class it with antimacassars, overmantels and other Victorian horrors, but really it is quite an attractive foliage plant. It is quite hardy in the south-west and I am growing it in a shady spot where I think its large green and white leaves will be a welcome and unusual feature.

Variegated *Tradescantia fluminensis*, which makes such attractive fillings for hanging baskets, is also good in a pot and the long trails that give it its name of Wandering Jew arrange themselves gracefully among the other plants. Its larger relation, *Zebrina pendula*, rather more fleshy and perhaps not quite so venturesome, also travels when it gets going, and is also called Wandering Jew. The Tradescant who brought these plants to England was the second gardener of that name. His father was gardener to Charles I.

I do not know when musk lost its perfume but I am sure the type that grew in pots in the cottage windows was scented because I know what the scent was like and I certainly have not savoured it for twenty years. Grown in a pot and given plenty of water musk made a very attractive window plant. This *Mimulus moschatus* had a pleasant scent one could only describe as 'musky' and we are told that at least during the last quarter-century no reliable records exist of wildlings so perfumed.

The large-flowered *Campanula isophylla* in white or blue is often used in hanging baskets, and it is just as pretty grown in a pot, for it tumbles over the edge in just the same way. It may not be hardy everywhere but I think it is hardier than people think. I know a garden near London where it has been growing happily in a hollow wall for many years, and I grow it out of doors in Somerset—in rather a sheltered spot, admittedly.

There is a little, striped aloe that I still see sometimes, *A. variegata*. The village name for it is Partridge Breast. I cannot remember whether the tender balsam, which is known as Busy Lizzie, had become popular in the days when cottages were cottages. I am sure it would have been a favourite, with its endless succession of bright red flowers dangling at the ends of the stems. I know that it was usual to grow mignonette in a pot so that it flowered at Christmas time. It was called Frenchman's Darling.

The cottagers did not always even trouble to pot their plants. A colchicum bulb lying on the window-sill was not unusual, and in due course it would produce its lilac flowers just as serenely as if it were growing in the garden. *Sauromatum guttatum* is another bulb that flowers without being planted. It is unusual rather than beautiful and is still being grown. It is not uncommon to read advertisements offering this 'Wonder Bulb' as Monarch of the East.

Sometimes there used to be a fly-trap in the window among the plants. Are there any of these old glass receptacles left now, I wonder?—with the lump of sugar at the bottom and the little cavity holding vinegar round the edge. They were typical of cottage rooms in the last century and went with the glass container of 'bee's wine' that stood on the mantelpiece. A middle-aged woman living in this village can remember just such a cottage with her great aunt sitting at the cottage door smoking a clay pipe!

19. A Cottage Nosegay

In London at the beginning of this century it was not unusual to see hand-carts piled high with bunches of cottage garden flowers—gay bunches of simple flowers, sweet williams and marigolds, stocks, cloves and rockets, with cornflowers, lupins and cabbage roses—all bunched together in the same effective but seemingly casual way in which they grow in their own gardens. They found ready purchasers in Hampstead and Kensington and were heralded as 'cottage bo-kays'. They were the same as the tight bunches of mixed flowers that were often seen packed into pails and displayed outside cottages in the country, to tempt the passer by. I still know one cottage where there are bunches of flowers for sale all through the summer. But it is motorists now, not walkers, who stop and buy the primroses, and scented nosegays.

The old term 'tussie-mussie' was used for the little bunches of flowers that came from cottage gardens to less fortunate friends living in towns. The spring mixture was bunch primroses (polyanthus), forget-me-nots and wallflowers, and later in the year the scented pinks and roses were mixed with the striped grass called Gardener's Garters, a few sprays of maidenhair fern or some spikes of lavender. Small children made their own little bunches to put on teacher's desk, and in cases of sickness or rejoicing the appropriate offering was always a bunch of flowers. Cottage gardeners were as generous with their flowers as the flowers were in their gardens.

For the last twenty years I have lived in a small village, and without exception the present that gives most pleasure is a gift of flowers. The giving is not all one-sided. I shall never forget a woman who was a complete stranger to me bringing a bunch of red tulips from her garden very soon after we had moved in. She lived in a cottage with a very small garden and it was a real sacrifice to pick so many of her tulips for a strange Londoner who had appeared in the village.

Flowers for the graves are more important than flowers in the home. I know that many of the flowers I give are taken up to the churchyard, and every Saturday I see scurrying figures, carrying flowers and jugs of water, making their way to the graves round the little church. The bunch of flowers is just as important as the pay packet to the girls who help in the house, and the burly stonemasons who are perpetually mending my walls or chimneys love to take home a bunch of flowers for the 'missus' on Saturday mornings.

Village life may change. The cottages and their gardens are different, but the love of flowers remains. The gardens may not be so tightly packed, but they are still gay with blossoms. The cottager now grows begonias, geraniums and dahlias, and the old flowers which he cherished for so many years are finding their way back to the larger gardens.

20. Autumn Tints

The typical flowers of autumn are chrysanthemums and so, of course, we find chrysanthemums in the little gardens as well as in the big ones. There are certain rather ordinary, good-tempered chrysanthemums that have come to be known as Cottage Pink or Cottage Bronze because at one time they were found in every cottage garden. Both have double flowers and are rather tall. They really need to be planted among other tall plants if they are to look attractive. The flowers are small in proportion to the long stalks, and if one can arrange it so that the flowers peep over the shoulders of other plants without showing too much of their bare and rusty stems, one likes them better. Cottage Bronze in particular needs this treatment, Cottage Pink is nearly as tall but has a sturdier stem. It is one of the last chrysanthemums to flower and there are usually flowers to pick up to the end of November.

Innocence is a pale single pink, very late in its flowering, and another of the hardy cottage chrysanthemums that can be treated like any other hardy perennial and left in the ground all through the year. The old Cottage Yellow is not very tall and is a pleasant not too strident colour.

It is a shame that so many of these old hardy chrysanthemums have disappeared. We still have Anastasia, the magenta-pink pompon, a bronze Anastasia, and a very pale pink of the same type. There is one of these pompons that seems to be a great favourite judging by the number of names it has. It is a pinkish-bronze, almost rose-madder, and it changes very pleasantly when it is going over. To me it is Dr Tom Parr because that was its name when I bought it. I have heard it called Dr Bob Parr, in another garden it goes by the name of Rob Roy, and it is, I think, the same as Mr Bowles' Bobby.

I wish I could find the name of a very unusual little chrysan-

114

themum that was given to me as Tiny, but it must have some
other name. It is tiny in every respect, barely a foot high, and
it covers itself with tiny typical chrysanthemum flowers. The
flowers are crimson with a golden eye, but not at all an ordinary
crimson. They have a glowing quality which is quite unlike that
of any plant I know, and looking at them from the other side of
the garden they shed a radiance which is quite uncanny. There
used to be many more of these hardy little chrysanthemums in
shades of pink and red, and they had romantic names such as
Mme du Barry and Madame de Pompadour, but I fear they are
not to be found today.

The michaelmas daisies that grew with the old chrysanthemums may not have been as large or as bright in colour as our
modern beauties but they had character. Climax is in a class by
itself and is still widely grown. No other daisy has such straight
stiff stems with perfect flowers regularly spaced. *Aster* Blue
Gown is newer, and it flowers a little later. The colour of the
flowers is deeper and they are not quite so neat, and though I do
grow it I would never oust Climax to make room for it or any
other of the modern types. The white counterpart of Climax,
Sam Banham, does still exist, but only just, and I fear his days
are numbered. I have it in the garden and I have to take great
care that it does not get removed by mistake because I know I
should never be able to replace it if that happened. The flowers
of St Egwyn are very small by modern standards but have a
lovely shade of pink which becomes almost luminous when it
catches the rays of the setting sun.

Some of the michaelmas daisies with very small flowers, such
as the cordifolius and ericoides types, are enjoying a come back
today in really lovely forms. There is one called Silver Spray,
another is Elegans, and they are improved versions of the old
favourites which had names like Ideal and Photograph. For
years I have treasured a dwarf michaelmas daisy with bronzed
foliage and it took me some time to discover the 'name', *A.
diffusus horizontalis* or more correctly *A. lateriflorus* var. *horizontalis*. The habit of the plant is low and spreading, and the
tiny lavender flowers with crimson centres, sit on top of the
stems. It does not increase with the rapidity of some of the
heartier asters and I watch it carefully to see it stays with me. It

is the kind of plant that might easily disappear if one did not check on it regularly. The stems get hard and woody and it makes little new growth, and I might easily lose it by being over generous. I always distribute my plants when I can because that is the way to make sure they do not die out. One can always ask for a bit back if one loses one's own plant, but the distributing habit has been my undoing more than once, when I have divided a plant beyond its endurance and left myself with a scrap too small to survive.

One of the last asters to flower and one of the most effective is *A. tradescantii*. This American species is very old, as one can tell by its name, and had rather dropped out of gardens until a few years ago when it showed signs of coming back into favour. I found my plant in a very modest little garden not far from my village, and now I wonder what I did before I had it. The foliage is as fine as asparagus and the little white daisies that nestle among it are good till the end. In so many asters the yellow centres turn brown before the petals of the flowers have faded, but those of tradescantii keep bright yellow to the end. It flowers so late that sometimes a frost will ruin the open flowers, but the unopened buds will open indoors if the graceful arching sprays are cut and brought inside.

I do not think *Parochetus communis* would be found in a normal English cottage garden, but it would be in an Irish one. Its names, St Patrick's Pea or Shamrock Pea suggest that. It needs moisture, a rich vegetable soil and a mild climate. When it has those three things it ramps away. I tried to grow it for years in my peat garden but dry summers killed it. Now, at last, I have established it in a north-facing bed in a mixture of green sand and peat, and there is no holding it back. I saw it doing even better in the peat walls in the Devonshire garden of a friend, but that garden is considerably damper than mine. Parochetus flowers very late with me. For some people it will start flowering in July but·for most of us it delays so long that one fears it is not going to flower at all, and then in late October or early November those brilliant blue pea-like flowers start to open and if the winter is kind they will be still at it at Christmas time. Even without the flowers I think parochetus is worth a struggle. The shamrock leaves are most beautifully marked with grey and crimson, and they vary with the seasons. As in clovers and other plants with three-foliate leaves these are neatly folded when they emerge, and at night they close themselves up neatly so that only the edges of the leaves are exposed to the cold, night air. I grow the red leaved clover, *Trifolium repens* var. *purpurascens*, for its rich foliage colour against the grey stones of my paving and that too puts itself to bed, folding its leaves back against the stem.

Brilliant blue flowers are not usual so late in the year, which makes the old-fashioned *Commelina coelestis* a favourite plant. Except in very favoured districts it is not hardy but it usually produces a few seedlings which can be grouped together to make a patch of vivid blue.

The old-fashioned white *Anemone japonica* is practically indestructible. It is sometimes difficult to establish but when the plants settle down you have them for life. The modern trend is to collect the coloured and double forms, the deeper the colour and the fuller the flowers the better we like them. *A. hupehensis* var. *elegans*, raised at Chiswick in 1848 is an attractive plant with pale rose flowers and a neat habit, and that would be my second love after the single white Japanese anemone of cottage gardens. There used to be a very good variety called Honorine Joubert, but the one I remember from my childhood and which is, I fear, getting scarce now, was just a white Japanese anemone— tall, lovely and flowering for weeks on end. I wonder why our modern gardeners who look for new plants to grow among shrubs do not plant white anemones? Of purest, glistening white, with golden centres, they would wander happily among the shrubs, bringing light and beauty with them.

Many sunflowers of one kind or another flower in the autumn, but the favourite of last century was usually referred to as Harpalium, a genus long ago included in helianthus. The plants had semi-double, bright yellow flowers and were favourites in the cottage gardens. They were mostly derived from *H. laetiflorus*, or *H. scaberrimus*, and from the former species was developed one named Miss Mellish, a cheerful, easy big daisy to brighten the autumn landscape.

The dahlias that were most popular were the pompon varieties in yellow or white, mauve or pink, or orange-yellow edged with crimson. Those neat, tightly-packed heads are just right for an old-world garden. Then there was a green dahlia, made up of green bracts, and looking rather like a small globe artichoke. It was rather untidy in growth, and sometimes tiny crimson petals appeared among the green but it was an unusual flower and much cherished. I have always had difficulty in keeping my dahlia tubers safe in winter. Whatever precautions I take they do not all survive and now I leave them in the ground and hope that they will survive. The cottagers have no such difficulties, they firmly bring their dahlias indoors for the winter and usually put them in the spare bedroom, and they always come through safely.

The good old *Sedum spectabile*, with its flat pink heads and succulent foliage is so good-tempered and generous that it is seen more often in small gardens than in big ones. Every little bit grows and the plant is most ornamental, even when not in flower. *Sedum spectabile* and the buddleias are the plants that bees and butterflies love best. There are better forms to be had today, Meteor with its deeper coloured flowers, Autumn Joy which is a pleasing blend of green, red and brown. *S. telephium* Munstead Red in warm shades of madder and crimson, has a slightly different habit of growth, with little bunches of flowers up the stems as well as the flat heads of flower. *Sedum maximum* var. *atropurpureum*, with its mahogany-coloured stems, leaves and flowers, makes a striking effect against a bank of silver foliage, but the cottage gardener does not worry about studied effects; his flowers arrange themselves, and they do so beautifully.

Index

119